Unveiling
Sophia

www.ChironPublications.com

Interior and cover design by Danijela Mijailovic

Printed primarily in the United States of America.

ISBN 978-1-63051-933-9 paperback
ISBN 978-1-63051-934-6 hardcover
ISBN 978-1-63051-935-3 electronic
ISBN 978-1-63051-936-0 limited edition paperback

Library of Congress Cataloging-in-Publication Data

Names: Taylor, Anne Elizabeth, author.
Title: Unveiling Sophia : heart wisdom in an age of technology / Anne Elizabeth Taylor.
Description: Asheville, N.C. : Chiron Publications, [2021] | Includes bibliographical references. | Summary: "Eternal feminine wisdom synchronizes the human heartbeat with the heartbeat of the universe. The Dalai Lama famously proclaimed that Western Women can save the world. But many modern women (and men) are painfully dissociated from Sophia, their inner spring of feminine wisdom and the primal source of their power and nurturance. Western women from around the globe have deep archetypal roots that have lain dormant after millennia of patriarchal control. Sophia awaits collective rebirth and her portal for rebirth is through the heart. Sophia, who the ancient Greeks regarded as the goddess of wisdom, represents a threshold through which we can access the deep reserves of archetypal wisdom veiled within our hearts"-- Provided by publisher.
Identifiers: LCCN 2021029808 | ISBN 9781630519339 (paperback) | ISBN 9781630519346 (hardcover) | ISBN 9781630519353 (ebook)
Subjects: LCSH: Wisdom--Religious aspects. | Heart--Religious aspects. | Heart--Symbolic aspects. | God--Wisdom. | Goddesses, Greek.
Classification: LCC BL65.W57 T39 2021 | DDC 204--dc23
LC record available at https://lccn.loc.gov/2021029808

Unveiling

Sophia

HEART WISDOM
IN AN AGE OF TECHNOLOGY

ANNE ELIZABETH TAYLOR, B.S., Ph.D.

Figure 1 Spiral relief, from Tarxien megalithic temple.
Image credit: Lenie Reedijk, taken in the Valletta Archaeological
Museum in Malta

Dedication

For Anna Kakalec Ruitberg

CONTENTS

LIST OF FIGURES

LIST OF PLATES

ACKNOWLEDGEMENTS

This book represents a personal alchemical process written over the course of several years. *Unveiling Sophia* and I evolved together and the archetypal Sophia was, as always, light years ahead of me. She consistently prodded or *hithered me on*, as Goethe might say. It is impossible for me to remember all the influences throughout the years, conscious and unconscious, that contributed to this book's evolution and birth. For all the subtle influencers along the way, I graciously thank you.

This book would not have been possible without Jody Bower who helped to shape its form and brought it into a state of readable "coherence."

I offer a heartfelt thank you to Dr. Sheldon Lewkis, who painstakingly read and provided valuable input prior to the book's final period of gestation. A sincere thank you to Dr. Ginette Paris who helped to shape and encourage my early work relating to the metaphorical heart, specifically during my writing of my doctoral dissertation, *Speaking to the Cardiologist through Myth and Metaphor*.

A special thanks goes out to Jennifer Fitzgerald at Chiron Publications and editor Robert Mikulak for their diligent work in facilitating the final stages of this book and the publication process itself.

A loving thank you to my children, Kimberly Thomas and Ian Thomas, for their unwavering belief, support, and encouragement throughout the writing of this book.

And lastly, a depth of my gratitude goes to Sophia Herself and the many guises She has embodied through the millennia. I heartfully acknowledge Sophia, Kundalini Shakti, the Virgin Mary, Mary Magdalen, and Anima Mundi (soul of the world) to name just a few.

INTRODUCTION

"I am the All. I am the Past, the Present, and the Future. No mortal has yet lifted my veil."[1]

— Isis

The focus of this book is on the heart and heart health from a perspective that transcends the causal dynamics of heart disease. I feel as if I've found an old trunk, thick with dust, that's been hidden in the basement of a house I came across in the deep woods. From the contents of this trunk, my focus includes the wisdom of the psyche, or soul, a wisdom that the ancient Greeks regarded as feminine and called *Sophia*.[2] Revitalizing the connection between heart and psyche restores our connection to the greater wisdom of the soul of the earth (the *anima mundi*) and the cosmos beyond. This connection enables us to see our world and our universe as not just complex, but as alive and purposeful: in the vocabulary used in this book, as ensouled and coherent. Sophia is the portal through which we can access the deep reserves of archetypal wisdom hidden within our hearts—the eternal feminine wisdom that synchronizes the human heartbeat with the heartbeat of the universe.

To reveal this wisdom, we must open ourselves to methods other than that of *logos*, the masculine principle of logic and structure that underlies the scientific approaches characteristic of our "enlightened" age. Spiritual practices such as meditation, somatic practices such as *Kundalini* yoga, and techniques for working with the deep psyche can unveil Sophia, reawakening our feminine wisdom. This applies

---

1   Inscription from the statue of Isis at Sais in ancient Egypt. Qtd. Steiner, R. *Isis, Mary, Sophia*, p. 20
2   To "love Sophia" (in the sense of a strong liking or affinity for, not romantic or erotic love) is the literal meaning of the word "philosophy," and such a philosophy is precisely what is needed in these pivotal times.

to both genders, for we all embody both masculine and feminine principles of psyche and soma.

Paradoxically, as we begin to lift her veil, we encounter scientific profundity, proving that masculine and feminine are not fundamentally at odds. Sophia does not replace *logos* but instead offers a balancing perspective, a wisdom beyond sense perceptions. Through her, the imaginative wisdom and inner knowing of the heart can allow us to move from scientism (the belief that science alone can provide meaning) to incorporate new forms of healing ourselves—and through our healing, heal the soul of the world, *anima mundi.*

Why I Wrote This Book

Even though we are born with open hearts, traumatic events and cultural immersion tends to "close down" the heart of many people, and so it was with me. A closed heart loses the ability to have compassion for self, others, and the world, resulting in a mindset of "me first." In an ego-centered state, we no longer hear the quiet voice of the heart that speaks in symbolic language over the noise of our "monkey mind" that never stops swinging from one thought to the next—primarily negative and self-defeating thoughts.

This book is, on one level, *my* story: the journey of transitioning from living a life based on hard science and logical thinking, career and financial security-focused, to a life that invites the mystery back in, a life that values direct experience and inner knowing. It is a life that values not only achievement but also fulfilment from living a heart-centered life. To make this journey, I traded in chemistry for alchemy, the accepted mechanized view of the heart for the imaginal heart, and my masculinized goal-setting self for the lost feminine aspects of my divine self. I discuss the more personal aspects of the closing of my heart in Chapter 5, "Descent to the Underworld."

When choosing a major for study in university, I resigned myself to pragmatic studies that my mother insisted I study: the sciences. Her generation experienced the Great Depression; it is understandable that she wanted the best for me and that she thought a stable career meant food on the table. Despite these good intentions, a part of my heart had to be silenced to proceed with a career path that was grounded mainly by pragmatism. My heart was not in it.

During my early working years, I was an electrocardiogram (ECG, sometimes written EKG) technician at our community hospital. There I encountered numerous "Code Blue" emergency events: the call for urgent medical assistance when someone is physiologically crashing and at risk of dying. I would hook up the heart monitoring electrodes to the patient in the midst of commotion as the clinicians worked to save the life of the patient. Watching a patient's heartbeat on the monitor go from highly irregular to flatline (no heartbeat) was a mesmerizing experience. Many times, hearts did not recover, and the patient faded away. But other hearts would spontaneously beat again. The same treatment protocols were applied, and yet it seemed to me that hearts had a *mind of their own* as far as the choice to come back to life—or not.

Repeatedly witnessing such an intense event had a profound effect on me, the wisdom of which would take years to unfold in my life. After decades of unfulfilling work, at midlife as so often happens, the discontent in me became so strong that I left an executive career in a heart monitoring device company and began my spiritual journey in a more deliberate way.

At first, this journey took the form of "dropping out" and opening an herb shop on an island accessible only by ferry. But I hungered to learn how other wisdom traditions understood the heart so that I could heal my heart that had long been silenced. Eventually I applied to a graduate program that would allow me to focus on the heart from a mythological and psychological perspective, including yogic practice. This was my personal journey to unveiling my own heart and seeking the voice of cosmic Sophia.

This journey has taught me that scientific knowledge *can* work together with wisdom from other disciplines to reveal levels of heart healing that include the physical, psychological, and spiritual. But first, we must unveil Sophia. I use the term *unveiling* as a metaphor that evokes the hiddenness of Sophia, the wisdom of the heart that serves as a portal and connects one to one's infinite nature. As Ibn Arabi describes Sophia in Llewellyn Vaughan-Lee's *Return of the Feminine*, she is "an image raising its head from the secrecy of the heart[3]."

Why We Need Sophia Now

> *Cardiovascular disease is the leading global cause of death, accounting for more than 17.9 million deaths per year in 2015, a number that is expected to grow to more than 23.6 million by2030.[4]* **(AHA 2018)**

Heart disease is a symptom of more systemic problems; it characterizes a collective disconnect from our hearts, personally, collectively, and ecologically. For the moment, I will discuss the physical ramifications of heart disease.

The statistics for diseases of the cardiovascular system are staggering:

- ♥ Cardiovascular disease accounts for nearly 836,546 deaths, approximately 1 of every 3 deaths, every year in the United States.

- ♥ About 2,300 Americans die of cardiovascular disease each day, an average of 1 death every 38 seconds.

- ♥ Cardiovascular diseases claim more lives each year than all forms of cancer and other smoking-related illnesses combined.

- ♥ About 92.1 million American adults are living with some form of cardiovascular disease or the after-effects of stroke. Direct and indirect costs of total cardiovascular diseases andstroke are estimated to total more than $329.7 billion; that includes both health expenditures and lost productivity.

---

3   Vaughan-Lee, Llewellyn. The Return of the Feminine and the World Soul. Point Reyes, CA: The Golden Sufi Center, 2009. P 189

4   American Heart Association: Heart Disease and Stroke Statistics. https://healthmetrics. heart.org/wp-content/uploads/2019/02/At-A-Glance-Heart-Disease-and-Stroke-Statistics-%E2%80%93-2019.pdf

♥ Cardiovascular disease is the leading global cause of death, accounting for more than 17.9 million deaths per year in 2015, a number that is expected to grow to more than 23.6 million by 2030.

In an age of unprecedented medical advances, from beta-blockers to routine heart transplants[5], heart disease[6] remains the number one killer of both men and women not just in the United States but worldwide, according to such authorities as the World Health Organization, the American Heart Association, and the Centers for Disease Control and Prevention.[7, 8] Western medicine has provided technological miracles that save countless lives from heart disease, yet little progress has been made toward solving the global heart disease epidemic. *Logos* by itself is failing us.

That is not to say that Western medicine is wrong. I spent years working in research and development for a major heart monitoring medical device company, and I value the contributions that science has made and continues to make. When someone experiences a heart attack[9], of course the first course of action is the emergency department of the nearest medical center.

If my own mother, who had rheumatic heart disease as a child, had lived just a while longer, she would have benefited from heart valve replacement technology. Sadly, her damaged heart gave out while she was still in her prime.

---

5   The Columbia University Medical Center reports that approximately 3,700 to 3,800 heart transplants are performed worldwide annually. http://columbiasurgery.org/heart-transplant/faqs Accessed Jul 16, 2018.

6   Including coronary heart disease, hypertension, and stroke.

7   https://www.who.int/news-room/fact-sheets/detail/the-top-10-causes-of-death

8   https://healthmetrics.heart.org/wp-content/uploads/2018/02/At-A-Glance-Heart-Disease-and-Stroke-Statistics- 2018.pdf

9   A heart attack occurs when a blood clot—usually resulting from atherosclerotic disease, a condition in which a mixture of hard fats and blood clots form plaques on artery walls—blocks an artery in the heart itself, preventing blood from getting to part of the heart muscle.

Western medicine shines when it comes to treating acute con-ditions that require immediate intervention. The job of the heart specialists, the cardiologists and cardiac surgeons is to "fix the pump" that moves the blood, with its life-giving oxygen and nutrients, throughout the body. Western medicine doesn't recognize the concept of *prana*, the Sanskrit term for life-force energy that rides on the wave of the breath. I will come back to this thread later. When their job is done, when the pump is put back together, the patient may be offered phys-ical rehabilitation and classes on healthy lifestyle changes. But who will pick up the pieces of the wounded psyche? How can the person best deal with the depression and questions about meaning that almost inevitably follow a heart attack? And who is doing something about the nonphysical factors that contribute to heart disease?

The term "Western medicine" is used in this book to denote the predominant mode of medical treatment, originating in the West and used throughout the world today. Western medicine is rooted in evidence-based theory; it is typically invoked only after people experience symptoms of a problem or measurable signs like elevated blood pressure or an irregular heartbeat. Numbers are the language of Western science. It relies on treatments that are typically administered externally, such as pharmacological (drug) treatment and surgery.

I contrast this approach with other healing methods that are experience-based and rely on the body's innate wisdom and ability to prevent and heal from disease states. These approaches are posited on the beliefs that disease typically begins long before symptoms manifest and that the causes of disease include psychological, ener-getic, and spiritual disturbances, all of which are interdependent. These approaches fall within a larger category that I call "Wisdom traditions," which also include what we term complementary or alternative medicine (CAM). Others have addressed the role of CAM in treating disease; my focus in this book is nonmedical forms of healing the heart.

In our postmodern culture, Western medicine often appears diametrically opposed to other methods, particularly those based on spiritual traditions. The basic premises of each seem to contradict each other. Spiritual approaches teach that at the core of knowledge lies an underlying unity, a sacred source, while Western science aims to break things down into smaller and smaller units of meaning, the "building blocks" of life.[10] Western science holds to the idea that there is a cause for all disease, and if a treatment can be found that eliminates or neutralizes that cause, healing will occur. So a disease state appears (the cause), which displays symptoms, and the treatment is applied. The effect of the treatment is the elimination of symptoms with the goal of healing. There is a direct relationship among symptom, treatment, and outcome. The relationship between cause and treatment is one-to-one, as shown in Figure 2.

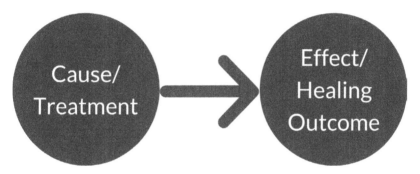

Figure 2 Evidence-based, one-to-one causal treatment dynamic. Image credit: author.

But in the other paradigm, the relationship shifts from a one-to-one repeatable protocol of cause and effect to a one-to-many relationship in which the desired outcome is achieved through various and divergent techniques.

From the standpoint of traditional methods, intervention can and should occur at an earlier stage. Once heart disease has progressed to being symptomatic, Western medicine is required to stabilize and

---

10   However, quantum physicists and neuroscientists confirm that the more one drills down to the smallest observable units, the more it is evident that there is an underlying unity to the universe and the mind. Renowned physicist and theorist David Bohm, said, "Deep down the consciousness of mankind is one. This is a virtual certainty because even in the vacuum matter is one; and if we don't see this, it's because we are blinding ourselves to it." (*The Essential Bohm*, p 149)

potentially reverse the condition. But Western medicine does not address the incidence of heart disease, nor does it provide adequate psycho-spiritual care after treatment. Western medicine works great for helping to make sure the body survives but does not address the whole person, especially the wounded psyche.

Wisdom approaches value heart-centered intuition, while Western science privileges reason. Western science relies on reproducible results, stating that proof lies in the ability to create the same results consistently, but the synchronistic or spiritual experiences central to Wisdom approaches cannot be repeated on demand and indeed, may be a once-in-a-lifetime event.

Western medicine has no room for spirituality; many scientists are openly dismissive of it, like evolutionary biologist and outspoken materialist Richard Dawkins, who sometimes sports a T-shirt emblazoned with the phrase "RELIGION: Together we can find a cure."[11] But it must be noted that the techniques discussed in this book are "spiritual but not religious"; they are not based on a particular creed, but rather on an underlying sense of a unity consciousness that transcends all religions.

By definition, if something is infinite, it cannot be fully defined or comprehended. We cannot, to give a purely mathematical example, ever complete the number Pi (Archimedes' constant); we cannot define the limits of our universe. If you don't believe that you are connected with infinity, then this book may not resonate with you. But if you have a sense that, in some way, you are connected to infinity, to something larger than yourself, then I believe the fundamental concepts presented in this book will be worthwhile considering whether you suffer from chronic stress, anxiety, heartbreak, or heart disease.

And despite these apparent oppositions, is it possible that we are missing a fundamental connection between the two approaches, Western and non-Western? What is lost when we address heart disease only through the Western scientific paradigm of the heart as a

---

11 https://www.spectator.co.uk/2014/08/the-bizarre-and-costly-cult-of-richard-dawkins/

pump, essentially a mechanical device with replaceable parts? Can we make room for another viewpoint that allows us to also address the heart as a dynamic part of our entire being?

It turns out that there is one approach that allows for such a melding of mindsets when it comes to treating heart disease: heart rate coherence.

Heart Rate Coherence:
The Bridge between Logos and Sophia

Heart rate coherence, synonymous with heart rhythm coherence, serves as a universal language that both scientists and Wisdom traditions may be able to agree upon. The HeartMath® Institute defines heart coherence as "a measure of the pattern in the heart's rhythm, which . . . reflects an orderly and harmonious synchronization among various systems in the body such as the heart, respiratory system and blood-pressure rhythms."[12] Heartbeats are not naturally regular; they do not occur in a rigid rhythm like the ticktock of a metronome. Instead, a normal heartrate has variation, usually imperceptible (but not always), yet measurable beat-to-beat variations.

Heart rate variations create dynamic rhythmic patterns in healthy people. In a healthy heart, *somatic coherence* dominates; this pattern takes on the form of a serpentine sine wave.[13] People with a healthy heart who are able to auto self-regulate their emotional responses to the inevitable stressors will likely have reasonably good heart rhythm coherence. Most of us don't. This has been my observation working with people over the years and researching medical literature.

While a person is under stress, habitually worried, living with high-functioning anxiety or has an unhealthy heart, the pattern appears chaotic. (Early pacemakers went the other way and caused the heart to beat too regularly, like a metronome, but the new smart

12   https://www.heartmath.org/support/faqs/research/
13   Depth psychology and spiritual approaches can also be described as using sine wave and spiral patterns, as we shall see.

pacemaker technology allows the heart to respond to breathing, mimicking a more natural heart rate rhythm.)

Bringing the physical heart and heart-wisdom together involves exploring and integration of the role of the body (*soma*) and its coherent operation, the soul (*psyche*) and its archetypal expressions, and spirit (*pneuma*), meaning connection to the coherent pulsation of the cosmos.

Heart rhythm coherence as measured by heart rate variability (HRV) is uniquely positioned to serve as a bridge between Western medicine and Wisdom approaches and yet is relatively underutilized in the Western medical community. This is hard for me to understand with statements such as the following example (of which there are many) in mainstream medical literature: "Low HRV is a harbinger of sudden death" ("The Broken Heart: Noninvasive Measurement of Cardiac Autonomic Tone"[14]).

Figure 3 demonstrates how the Wisdom traditions approach healing, using heart rhythm coherence (using their own equivalent terminology) as the central focus. In this paradigm, disease states and symptoms may be prevented or treated by contemplative practices (mindfulness[15], yoga, tai chi, etc.) that have been demonstrated in studies to contribute to heart coherence. There is no one single treatment that consistently produces the goal of high heart coherence, no one right path. Treatment is person-centered, experiential, *yet quantifiable.*

This book begins with a discussion of how Western medicine views the heart and the current state of medical treatment for heart disease. The next section focuses on heart rhythm coherence itself and the dynamics of the autonomic nervous system.

Using heart coherence as the bridge, the following chapters cover examples of the somatic practices that allow a person to achieve and

---

14   Oppenheimer S. (1992). The broken heart: noninvasive measurement of cardiac autonomic tone. *Postgraduate medical journal, 68*(806), 939–941. https://doi.org/10.1136/pgmj.68.806.939
15   Mindfulness means "paying attention in a particular way: on purpose, in the present moment, and non- judgmentally." (Kabat-Zinn, 1990)

maintain health without external interventions. While there are many such practices, in this book I focus primarily on how a daily practice of *Kundalini* yoga[16] or meditation can affect heart rate variability, which is a major predictor of overall health as well as heart health.

Next, the narrative moves from soma to psyche. The chapter on psyche is based on depth psychological approaches drawn from the theories of C. G. Jung and later Jungian theorists.

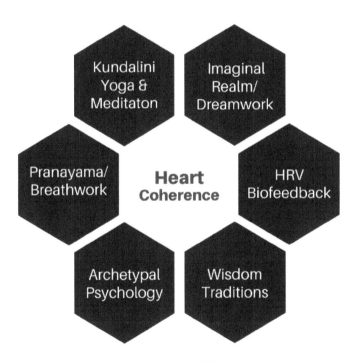

Figure 3 A many-to-one dynamic with heart coherence as healing unitive center. Image Credit: Author created using Canva.

---

16   *Kundalini* yoga is just one of many schools of yoga. Most, if not all yoga traditions, utilize *kundalini* energy. It is the yoga that I, the author, have been practicing for many years. Other forms of yoga are as, and possibly more, effective than *Kundalini* yoga.

Depth psychology refers to the deep or unconscious psyche, that which we access primarily in dreams, meditation, and trance states. A basic premise of depth psychology is that unresolved psychological issues often manifest themselves as disease states. Building on this platform, I then focus on spiritual approaches to healing.

In each section, the balance between masculine and feminine forces comes into play and reveals its central importance. The interplay of masculine and feminine dynamics implicitly relates to heart rhythm coherence as well as the psyche and spirit in heart health and disease.

From there, I explore the archetypal symbols of the coherent heart, such as the sine wave, circle, spiral, helix, star, temple, and snake, and their significance in relation to the heart.

Archetypes may be thought of as psychic seeds, as image and pattern generators, inherited and collectively shared among humans irrespective of time and culture. Archetypal images such as the caduceus/snake, which dates back to ancient cultures such as the Sumerian, Chinese, Egyptian, and Mesoamerican are as relevant today as they have been in the past, particularly when working with imagery as an artist and as a means for exploring the psyche, soma, and spirt.

The Physical Heart

CHAPTER ONE

Coming to Understand the Heart

"Nature is simple, but scientists are complicated[17]."
— Francisco Torrent-Guasp

Our ideas about the heart have changed through the centuries—and continue to change. Some theories about the heart and circulation from the last two millennia have been discarded and now are coming back around. New theories have also emerged, demonstrating the elegance and simplicity of nature, and like it or not, we are still a part of nature. Some theories have been proven wrong, as emergent research demonstrates. I'll begin the discussion with Galen.

Pre-Enlightenment Ideas About the Heart's Structure and Function

Galen (Claudius Galenus), who lived from 129 to 200 C.E., at the height of the Roman Empire, is known as the "Father of Medicine." He was the emperor's personal physician and an anatomist who gained his knowledge of human anatomy by serving as surgeon to the gladiators in Pergamon. He believed that the best doctors were also philosophers, and his own philosophy included the Hippocratic and Aristotelian idea of vitalism. Vitalism was based on Plato's idea that *pneuma* (a Greek

---

17 Qtd. Buckberg, G. "Basic science review: The helix and the heart." *J Thorac Cardiovasc Surg* 2002;124:863-83.

word meaning breath, wind or spirit, analogous to *spiritus* in Latin[18]) was "the vital principle by which the body is animated."[19, 20] The notion of vitalism is to be underscored as a theory that went out of fashion and is now making its orbital return.

Vitalism sprang from the worldview that everything on earth has a soul but can be differentiated according to reasoning ability, as argued by Hermias in Plato's *Phaedrus*. Hermias lays out these distinctions: ". . . there are three ensoulments, and each differs from the other. The soul enters and ensouls first the ethereal vehicle, then the pneumatic vehicle, and finally the corporeal body."[21] The pneumatic vehicle is "the seat of images rather than thoughts," a concept that will play into later chapters of this book.

The three types of ensoulments relate, respectively, to air, water, and earth. *Pneuma* serves as the intermediary between the noncorporeal soul and the physical body, and its nature is liminal. Plato believed that there were three levels of *pneuma*: 1. inhaled on the breath from the divine; 2. activating the alimentary canal; and 3. transforming in the heart to its highest form, the vital spirit animating the body. Plato may have been influenced in this idea by his contemporary, the philosopher and medical theorist Alcemaeon of Croton, who posited that *pneuma* circulated through the arteries.

Aristotle condensed this theory to the idea that natural bodies consist of the substance or matter—the physical body itself—and soul, which determined the form of the matter. The soul, in other words, determined what form a being would take and was inseparable from the body.

---

18   *Prana* in Sanskrit, *ruah* in Hebrew, *rūh* in Arabic; however, there are nuances to all these terms that precludethem being used as exact synonyms (discussed in later chapters).

19   *Thayer's Green Lexicon* (1911).

20   Bechtel, William and Robert C. Richardson. "*Vitalism*." In: Taylor and Francis, eds. *Routledge Encyclopedia of Philosophy*, 1998, doi:10.4324/9780415249126-Q109-1. https://www.rep.routledge.com/articles/thematic/vitalism/v-1.

21   Finamore, John F. "Hermias and the Ensoulment of the Pneuma."

Physicians of the time worked from the premise that healing meant working with divine energies. The original Hippocratic oath required of all physicians before they could start practicing began thusly: "I swear by Apollo the Healer, by Asclepius, by Hygeia, by Pancea, and by all the gods and goddesses, making them my witnesses, that I will carry out, according to my ability and judgment, this oath and this indenture." The gods and goddesses were not only present but necessary to healing.

Galen believed that vital spirits create heat and that "the heart is . . . the heartstone and source of the innate heat by which the animal is governed."[22] Religious mandates of Galen's day did not allow surgical experiments on human corpses, so Galen's research on the heart was primarily limited to dissecting animals. He found that the arteries are full of blood, which he thought was generated by the liver and "spun out" to the body where needed through the heart, where it was mixed with *pneuma*. He saw the flow of blood through the arteries as motivated by a kind of centrifugal force, which ebbed and flowed rather than circulated.[23] Galen speculated that the organs "attracted" blood as needed.

Galen theorized that blood flows through the arteries, but he conceived the venous blood as moving through "invisible pores" across the septum, the wall (in today's worldview) that divides the chambers of the heart. Galen's theory held for 1,500 years—until Harvey's groundbreaking work shifted the paradigm.

---

22 Qtd https://web.stanford.edu/class/history13/earlysciencelab/body/heartpages/heart.html

23 The Center for Vascular Biology Research, Department of Medicine, Beth Israel Deaconess Medical Center and Harvard Medical School, Boston, MA, USA. William Cameron Aird, M.D. Professor of Medicine

Harvey and the Enlightenment

William Harvey published *De Motu Cordis* in 1628. This book revolutionized the understanding of the heart and circulation by introducing his theory on "the motion of the heart and the blood in living creatures," which he formulated through empirical observation and reason.[24] Harvey's theory forms the basis of what is taught in medical schools today, however, as we shall see in the segment titled "Emerging Paradigms," this may soon change.

Harvey's theory described the circular movement of the blood in a closed system or continuous loop, explaining how blood is sent from the heart through the aorta with each heartbeat. Harvey summed up his discoveries as follows: "These points being proved, I conceive it will be manifest that the blood circulates, revolves, is propelled, and then returning from the heart to the extremities, from the extremities to the heart, and thus that it performs a kind of circular movement."[25]

However, Harvey did not challenge the theory of ensoulment. Indeed, "for a period of time, he continued to espouse an essentially vitalistic and qualitative picture of the human body,"[26] particularly that the blood mixed with *pneuma*. Thus, Harvey was the bridge between the ancient, "ensouled" view of the body and modern medicine. Thomas Wright notes in his biography of Harvey that:

> Harvey's masterpiece [*De Motu Cordis*] can be enjoyed not only as an account of his researches . . . but also as a fine and fascinating work of seventeenth-century literature and philosophy. His clear, vivid prose returns us to a time in which 'science' was a sister study to 'humanities' disciplines, and benefited profoundly from that close relationship.[27]

---

24 Thomas Wright, *William Harvey: A Life in Circulation*. Worth reading for a more thorough account of William Harvey and his predecessors.
25 Powers
26 Aird, 2011, p. 124
27 Wright, op. cit.

Harvey's work was a mix of *logos* and Sophia. It would attract criticism on both counts.

First, as Casper Hofmann, a professor of medicine and contemporary of Harvey, pointed out, Harvey could neither explain nor demonstrate how the arteries and veins were connected, thereby making it difficult to accept his theory of a closed circulation system. The microscopes enable scientists to see the capillaries that form a bridge between arteries and veins would not be invented until 1681; only then could Harvey's theory be validated. Harvey intuited the invisible connection of arteries and veins before the tools of *logos*, the instrumentation that can see and measure, existed. As is often the case in science, the feminine voice of intuition preceded our ability to empirically prove something through reason alone. Using this new tool, the microscope, Marcello Malpighi, a professor of anatomy often called the father of microanatomy, was able to confirm that capillaries were the "invisible" connection Harvey claimed must exist.

A more severe condemnation offered by Hofmann was that the circulation lacked purpose. Hofmann thought Harvey's theory needed to explain what end the circulatory system serves—what does it do for the body? Harvey admitted that he did not adequately answer this question. But he stuck to his intuitive feeling that there was a purpose behind the system, reiterating that "The heart is the tutelary deity of the body, the basis of life, the source of all things, carrying out its function of nourishing, warming, and activating body as a whole." The beauty of Harvey's description exemplifies a mindset that simultaneously holds both possibilities, science and spirituality. Like Galen, Harvey believed that the heart generates heat. He described the relationship between the heart and the sun, including its ability to radiate heat. The archetypal significance of the heart as the central sun of the body further elevates its importance beyond a blood pump. He affirmed that

> ... The animal's heart is the basis of its life, its chief member, the sun of its microcosm; on the heart all its activity depends, from the heart all its liveliness and strength arise.

> Equally is the king the basis of his kingdoms, the sun of his microcosm, the heart of the state; from him all power arises and all grace stems.[28]

Harvey sensed that life itself, for humans and animals, depended upon the heart more than any other organ. Despite that fact that his theory was incomplete from a logistical and philosophical standpoint, *De Motu Cordis* is still considered today to be one of the most influential books in medicine. And in due time, physicians would come to understand the necessary role that circulation plays in maintaining life and health.

Harvey's theory found an ally in René Descartes, the French philosopher and mathematician. But this ally was also responsible for expunging Harvey's ideas of vitalism. Descartes took Harvey's assertion that "it is by the heart's vigorous beat that the blood is moved, perfected, activated, and protected from injury and coagulation"[29] to promulgate his own interpretation of the heart as a mechanized pump, one devoid of the ineffable energies of *pneuma* so important to Hippocrates, Aristotle, and Galen—and to Harvey.

Thus, Harvey's work occupied the liminal space between a world that people saw as ensouled and the emerging idea that the world is purely mechanical, the primary assumption that would characterize the Scientific Revolution. Descartes refocused Harvey's findings in language reflecting the new zeitgeist, which continues to reign to this day as the primary paradigm in the Western psyche. For example, Descartes wrote the following about Harvey in his book titled *Discourses:*

> I need give no other answer than what has already been written by an English physician, to whom homage must be paid for having broken the ice in this area, and for being the first to have taught that there are many small passages at the extremities of the arteries through which the blood they

---

28 Ibid.
29 Ibid

receive enters into the small branches of the veins, from which it flows immediately to the heart, so that its course is merely a perpetual circulation.[30]

The mutation of Harvey's vitalist theory into Descartes' purely mechanical notion is symbolic of the critical bifurcation of spirit and matter that has dominated Western thought since the 17th century. The propensity of the Western mind to feel the need to extract what if perceives to be the essence or essential point does so at the expense of the greater truth or whole. Descartes extracted the soul from the heart, perhaps even single-handedly.

Vitalism was "usurped from the throne," as Carl Jung might have phrased it, along with the idea that the divine plays a role in healing. Physicians taking the Hippocratic oath have dismissed the gods and goddesses who have now gone underground. "I will respect the hard-won scientific gains of those physicians in whose steps I walk, and gladly share such knowledge as is mine with those who are to follow.[31]" Human physicians are now the gods of healing and appeal to each other as their sources of help.

As the "enlightened" perspective focused more and more on science as the only true form of knowledge, other forms of experiential and intuitive knowing became excluded from our understanding of the heart. The new mechanistic model excludes both soul/psyche and Sophia, intuitive heart wisdom. While it has increased our understanding of *how* the natural world works, it has neglected the *why* and thus greatly contributed to the worldwide epidemic of anxiety, depression, and general psychological malaise. Yet the mysteries of the heart were far from being solved. Indeed, the heart's structure was described as the "Gordian knot of Anatomy" in 1864 by Scottish anatomist James Bell Pettigrew, who won an Anatomy Gold Medal for his work on the nervous system of the heart. The Gordian knot

---

30   René Descartes, *Discourses*, p. 51.

31   Written in 1964 by Louis Lasagna, Academic Dean of the School of Medicine at Tufts University, and used in many medical schools today. https://www.pbs.org/wgbh/nova/article/hippocratic-oath-today/#modern

is a metaphorical term for an unsolvable puzzle dating back to the times of Alexander the Great (356-323 B.C.E.). One of Pettigrew's key theories was that movement in the animal and plant systems was often spiral and helical, "especially of the voluntary and involuntary muscles, as seen in . . . the ventricles of the heart." Figure 4 shows Pettigrew's diagram of the heart muscles.

Although Pettigrew's theory is not well known in Western medical circles, it plays a critical role in our understanding of the anatomical heart. The spiral muscle formation theory of the early 20th century will be revisited when I discuss the work of Francisco Torrent-Guasp which further demonstrates the spiral theory.

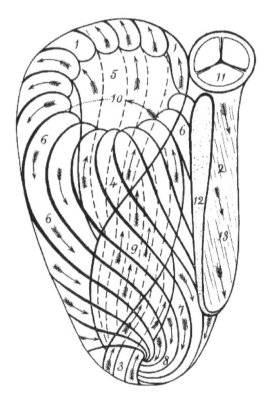

Figure 4 Pettigrew's diagram showing the spiral musculature of the heart (Open Source: Pettigrew, J. Design in Nature. Longmans Green: London, 1908. Page 32).

Emerging Paradigms

Theories about the heart have continued to evolve and morph. Several years ago, I encountered Rudolph Steiner's assertion that the heart is *not* a pump and that it is the blood the causes the heart to beat and not the other way around.[32] Put another way, the heart is just one component of the complex circulatory system, not the center of it. This statement by Steiner, a scientist, philosophical scholar, and writer, struck me with the force of a kōan[33]. In my search to find answers, I came across the work of physician Thomas Cowan,[34] whose research explores Steiner's notion of the heart being analogous to a "hydraulic ram" rather than a pump, in that the heart actually *stops* the blood flow, allowing it to collect before pumping it on.

Another medical researcher, cardiothoracic surgeon Gerald Buckberg[35], has found that an important function of the heart is to put a "spin" on the blood, to create spiral flow versus laminar flow.[36] Laminar flow is defined as the smooth flow of a fluid in layers that do not mix. It can be visualized as the flow in a river: The water travels faster and straighter in the middle than at the river's edge, where swirling patterns occur because of the interference of the river bank.

For a long time, laminar flow was how people visualized the flow of blood in arteries and veins. But we are now realizing that in healthy people, blood flow has a distinctive spiral flow pattern, while the blood flow in people with unhealthy hearts loses this spiral pattern.

---

32   Rudolf Steiner (1861-1925), an Austrian philosopher, social reformer, scientist, and esoteric thought leader, was a key figure in the popularization of biodynamic agriculture, educational principles adopted by the Walden Schools, and his theories on the heart.

33   A paradoxical riddle used by Zen Buddhist monks in meditation to provoke realization of hidden higher truths.

34   Incidentally also an expert on Steiner's spiritual science, anthroposophy (a word based on *anthropo*, human, and Sophia, wisdom).

35   Gerald Buckberg (born September 29, 1935) is a Distinguished Professor of Surgery, Division of Cardiothoracic Surgery, at the David Geffen School of Medicine at UCLA.

36   Buckberg 2002.

An important theorist in this area was the 20th-century Spanish cardiologist and anatomist Francisco Torrent-Guasp, who spent over 25 years trying to solve the mystery of the heart's architecture. Torrent-Guasp discovered the true structure of the heart by literally "untying" or unwrapping a bovine heart with his hands. After boiling a bovine heart and removing the major vessels, he was able to unfold the heart's ventricles into one continuous, band-shaped muscle.[37]

This physical geometry of the heart has a lot to do with its efficient spiraling of blood. Not only does the human heart beat in a rhythmic sine wave pattern when in coherence, but the heart muscle itself forms two reciprocal spirals (spirals within spirals) that terminate in a helix at a fixed apex. Reciprocal spirals occur when one spiral goes clockwise while the opposing one goes counterclockwise, as in the horns of a ram. Reciprocal spiraling increases both strength and movability and is plentiful throughout nature.[38]

Torrent-Guasp first published his revolutionary concepts of cardiac anatomy and its function in 1973. Torrent-Guasp found that the reciprocal spiral structure of the heart causes the ejection and suction phase of the heartbeat through a twisting and untwisting motion. The heart, in other words, twists in a spiral movement to facilitate the movement of blood. Then as the heart relaxes and untwists, a suction is created that pulls blood into the heart again. This discovery contradicts Harvey's notion of the way the heart fills and empties. As Buckberg notes, the ancient Greeks, with their idea of the ebb and flow of the blood, had a better sense of the basic biological functioning of the heart than Harvey.[39]

Buckberg confirmed Torrent-Guasp's theory using magnetic resonance imaging (MRI) to watch the heart in action. Again, sophisticated

---

37 Francisco Torrent-Guasp discusses the heart's anatomy and demonstrates the techniques he used in his discovery of the helical structure of the heart in this video: https://youtu.be/N6ORMHi9rcU

38 The uterus also works on this principle; it has several layers of muscles, two of which overlap each other in a crisscross pattern, greatly increasing the power of the organ during labor.

39 Buckburg, *The Helix and the Heart*, 2002.

instrumentation followed intuitive knowledge of the structure and function of the heart. Buckberg also found that in heart failure, the heart often loses its healthy helical apex; instead of resembling the end of a football, a heart in failure often takes on the spherical shape of a basketball, making it less able to twist efficiently.

We are coming ever closer to understanding the healthy heart. And part of that new understanding involves the idea of the coherent heart.

EXPERIENTIAL PRACTICE

"Cardiac Dance: The Spirals of Life"

"The Cardiac Dance: The Spirals of Life" was a creative collaboration between cardiologist Gerald Buckberg, executive producer, and the University of Cincinnati's College-Conservatory of Music, demonstrating Torrent-Guasp's theory that the heart exists as spirals within spirals. The original live performance was choreographed by Shellie Cash[40] and took place in May 2007.

The dance takes place in five acts. It celebrates the heart's healthy, harmonic movement; shows the irregularity of form after a heart attack; and expresses how heart surgery can restore the spiral function of the heart leading to resuscitation and rebirth. For this exercise, go to https://youtu.be/ckjzEJsFjHE and watch the dance performance.[41]

Allow the images and spiraling formations of the dancers to reach beyond your rational mind into the depths of psyche. After watching the dance, spend some time writing your associations and amplifications of the images in a journal.

---

40 For a complete list of full cast and crew visit https://www.imdb.com/title/tt5171898/fullcredits/?ref_=tt_ov_st_sm
41 Uploaded by the David Geffen School of Medicine UCLA

CHAPTER TWO

The Beating Heart

"A healthy heart is not a metronome[42]."

Before we can relate the idea of coherence to the heart, a few basics about how the heart works must be explained.

The Heartbeat

A beating heart physically contracts, then expands, as Harvey's theory stipulates, creating a rhythmic oscillation that can be felt as your pulse or a "lub-dub" pulsation at the wrist or in the chest. Incredibly, the heart beats approximately 85,000 to 100,000 times a day. All parts of the body feel the ebb and flow of this perpetual pulsation even though we are not typically aware of it consciously. The pulsating heart is one form of somatic communication where the undulations are felt throughout the body.

The "lub-dub" sensation is what we feel when the upper chambers of the heart (the atria) contract, followed by the stronger contraction of the lower chambers (the ventricles). The current theory of circulation teaches that oxygenated blood flows from the left atria to the left ventricle, then through the aorta, the largest blood vessel.

---

42   Shaffer, F., McCraty, R., & Zerr, C. L. (2014). A healthy heart is not a metronome: an integrative review of the heart's anatomy and heart rate variability. *Frontiers in Psychology, 5,* 1040. doi:10.3389/fpsyg.2014.01040

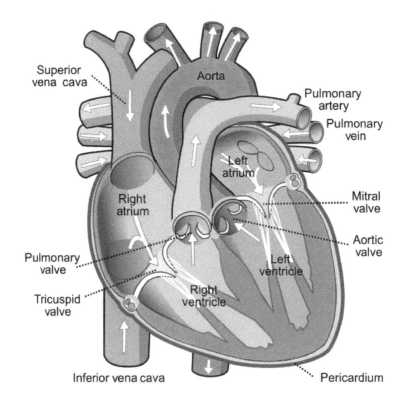

Figure 5 Circulation & the Heart. Image Credit: Creative commons.[43]

From there, blood flows through smaller arteries out into the body and organs, where it brings oxygen and nutrients to all the cells. It then returns through the veins to the right atrium. When the right atrium contracts, the blood flows into the right ventricle, which pulsates it into the vessels and capillaries of the lungs. There, the blood eliminates carbon dioxide (which we exhale) and picks up a fresh load of oxygen. It then flows back to the left atrium and down to the left ventricle, and the cycle repeats.

---

43   By Wapcaplet - Own work, CC BY-SA 3.0, https://commons.wikimedia.org/w/index.php?curid=830253

The Electromagnetic Field

The heart has the unique ability to generate its own electricity; this is known as the heart's intrinsic conduction system. The system includes cells (myocytes) that generate an electrical impulse and cells that transmit this impulse through the heart muscle.

Each heartbeat is initiated by an electrical signal generated by the heart's natural pacemaker, the sinus atrial (SA) node, located in the wall of the right atrium. The "firing" of the SA node initiates a chain of reactions: first, the upper heart chambers (the atria) contract, which stimulates the atrial ventricular (AV) node after a brief delay allowing the atria to completely empty. The AV node then fires and causes the lower heart chambers (the ventricles) to contract.

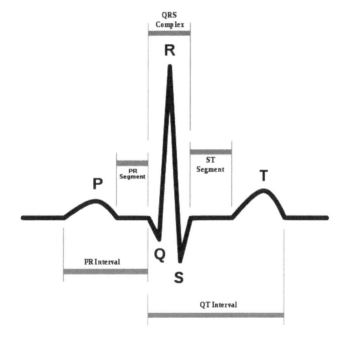

Figure 6 Schematic representation of normal ECG.[44] Image credit: Created by Agateller (Anthony Atkielski), converted to svg by atom., Public domain, via Wikimedia Commons.

---

44   https://commons.wikimedia.org/wiki/File:SinusRhythmLabels.svg

The electrical current generated by the heart also travels to the surface of your skin (and beyond), where it can be measured using electrodes to generate an electrocardiograph (ECG), a recording of the electrical current flowing through the heart. When medical personnel look at an ECG, they are assessing the morphology or shapes of the waveform; the four main components are the P wave, QRS complex, ST segment, and T wave. Other components such as the ST segment and U wave are beyond the scope of this elementary discussion.

P Wave

When the SA node (pacemaker) fires, it causes a shift in the electrical state of the myocytes. The cells become less negatively charged, which causes the muscle to contract. This shift shows up as the P wave on ECG.

QRS

The electrical impulse moves along the pathways between the SA node and the AV node.

The AV node slows the electrical flow, allowing time for the atria to completely contract and empty of blood, before the signal travels along the ventricular conductive pathway known as the bundle of His. From there, the signal moves to each ventricle and down to the apex of the heart, causing the ventricles to contract and eject blood out to the body through the aorta. These movements are shown on ECG as the QRS complex.

T Wave

As the heart beats, the atria repolarize (positive ions build up again) and relax, then the ventricles follow. This can be seen on the ECG as the T wave. Each cycle generates a unique QRS complex (the blips on the line in the graph), separated by time intervals, as shown in Figure 7.

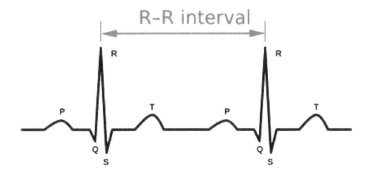

Figure 7 Normal QRS complexes shown on electrocardiogram with R-R interval highlighted. Image Source: Public Domain.[45]

Because it works on electricity, the heart also generates an electro-magnetic field (sometimes called an oscillating field). This field has been measured up to 8 feet or more from the body using a supercon-ducting quantum interference device first developed in the 1970s (see Figure 8). Researchers at the HeartMath® Institute have found that the electromagnetic field of the heart is approximately 60 times stronger than that of the brain waves recorded by electroenceph-alogram (EEG—a measure of the electrical activity of the brain).[46] Like all electromagnetic fields, this oscillating field interacts with its environment, both the interior and exterior of the body.

---

45   https://commons.wikimedia.org/wiki/File:ECG-RRinterval.svg
46   McCraty, Rollin. HeartMath® researcher.

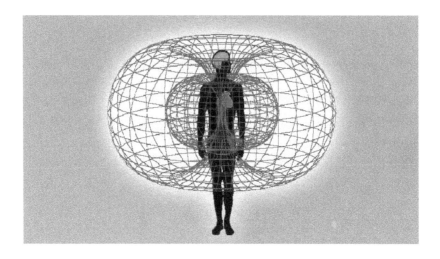

Figure 8 The electromagnetic field.
Image credit: public domain.[47]

The interaction of overlapping oscillating fields will be key as this discussion continues. Such interaction can be better understood by example, pendulum clocks. Multiple experiments have demonstrated that if one sets several pendulums in motion (within close proximity of each other) the weaker pendulums will eventually sync up with the strongest pendulum. Similarly, because its field is strongest, the heart functions as the conductor of the other oscillating fields of the human body. The weaker electromagnetic fields within the body sync up with the heart's frequency patterns. A heart in coherence, in balance, can also affect the hearts of others nearby. Yet the heart is also subject to oscillating fields from outside the body such as the Earth's electromagnetic field. Thus, the heart is an intermediator organ: It "leads" the body's rhythmic pulsations and affects nearby hearts, but in turn it is led by forces beyond the body, including the earth, sun, and cosmos. A healthy heart syncs up its electromagnetic filed to the Earth, which in turn is affected by the sun and beyond.

---

47   By http://uniteunderfreedom.com/?p=1006; http://uniteunderfreedom.com/?p=1006, Public Domain, https://commons.wikimedia.org/w/index.php?curid=22685038

The Neurological System

To understand heart coherence more fully, it is necessary first to understand the autonomic nervous system (ANS). The ANS controls body functions that operate "automatically," below your conscious awareness. For example, digestion happens whether you think about it or not. Some functions, like breathing, are mostly autonomic—a good thing, as you can go to sleep trusting that you will keep on breathing— but you can also consciously choose to alter your breathing patterns and thereby directly impact your ANS, including heart rate.

Sympathetic and Parasympathetic Systems

The ANS has two major subdivisions: the sympathetic and the para-sympathetic branches. The sympathetic nervous system controls the "flight or fight" response. When we are stressed or frightened, it causes our muscles to tense up and the heart rate to speed up, getting us ready to run away or to stand and fight. The parasympathetic nervous system controls what is referred to as "rest and digest" responses by causing muscles to relax and the heart rate to slow. As with breathing, people can learn to self-regulate and override the sympathetic nervous system through training such as meditation and thus allow the parasympathetic branch to return to a balanced state.

Our bodies are designed to become supercharged for survival during a stressful event. However, the body does not differentiate between types of stress. Neurologically, we react the same way to being chased by a tiger, a near-miss auto accident, a demanding boss, or unrelenting financial pressures because the sympathetic branch dominates.

Most Western people suffer from sympathetic branch domination due to chronic stress, anxiety, and limited time to relax. But complete relaxation is not the optimum state either. The fairy tale of *Goldilocks and the Three Bears* illustrates this issue. Papa Bear symbolizes the sympathetic nervous system, whose reactions can make us faster, harder, and hotter. Mama Bear symbolizes the parasympathetic nervous system, which makes us slow down, soften, and cool off.

In stressful situations, Papa Bear rules, and in relaxation mode, Mama Bear rules. Baby Bear symbolizes the *just right* zone where neither is dominant. We are healthiest when the ANS is balanced: not static, always changing, but moderating the mix so that it does not get too hot or too cold, too hard or too soft.

The All-Important Vagus Nerve and the Polyvagal Theory

While the SA node controls heart rate (how often the heart beats), the parasympathetic system slows the heart through the action of the vagus nerve. The vagus nerve is a paired cranial nerve, one branch for each side of the body (10th cranial nerve). *Vagus* is Latin for "wanderer," and it meanders throughout the body and provides two-way communication (motor and sensory) between the brain and the rest of the body. Originating within the base of the brain, the pair descends on either side of the neck, affecting speech and the voice, continuing through the thorax where they connect to most of the organs of the body, and end at the pelvic floor. The right vagus nerve innervates the SA node, the heart's intrinsic or natural pacemaker, and serves to lower heart rate.

Stephen W. Porges introduced the Polyvagal Theory[48] in 1994, contributing an innovative perspective linking autonomic function to human behavior.[49] According to the Polyvagal Theory, the ANS is a hierarchical system with two vagal motor systems, the ventral vagus nerve and the dorsal vagus nerve. The ventral vagus nerve (sometimes referred to as new vagus nerve[50]) is higher up on the evolutionary timeline. It's a myelinated,[51] or insulated, nerve that

---

48   Stephen W. Porges is a "Distinguished University Scientist" at the Kinsey Institute, Indiana University Bloomington, and professor in the department of psychiatry at the University of North Carolina in Chapel Hill in North Carolina.

49   Porges SW. Orienting in a defensive world: Mammalian modifications of our evolutionary heritage: A Polyvagal Theory. Psychophysiology. 1995;32:301–318. [PubMed] [Google Scholar]

50   Rosenberg, Stanley. Accessing the healing power of the vagus nerve, 13.

51   Myelination is a protective fatty coating or insulation that speeds nerve transmission.

originates in the brain and ends below the heart, above the diaphragm (supradiaphragmatic). The unmyelinated dorsal vagus nerve pathway (old vagus nerve) is primitive; it continues from below the diaphragm, regulates digestion and other functions below the diaphragm.

Porges' Polyvagal theory hypothesizes that the autonomic nervous system will respond to external stimuli, safety or danger, in a predictable and hierarchical manner[52]: 1) ventral vagus nerve associated with positive social engagement; 2) dorsal vagus nerve (fight/flight); and 3) sympathetic activity of spinal chain (immobilization/freezing), the last being potentially life-threatening (as in stopping the heart). The immobilization, or freeze phase of the autonomic response, goes beyond the heretofore accepted theory of fight/flight only. Think of the last time you were criticized by someone. Your first reaction may be to call a friend who hopefully empathizes and sooths us (ventral vagus) by offering supportive comments. If that tactic fails (your friend was unavailable or in a bad mood), you may fight back with your own verbal defense or "run away" from the conversation (sympathetic branch). The body does not differentiate between life-threatening attacks and those that just feel that way. If the second tactic doesn't work, you may actually "freeze up" or dissociate in order to protect yourself from harm (dorsal vagus).

Porges' work linking specific ancient ritual activities with associated vagal response provides a linchpin between Ancient Wisdom practices or rituals and his Polyvagal theory. This is critically important because when we measure vagal tone (the health of the vagus nerve), we can validate the effectiveness of specific spiritual practices. Vagal nerve tonality is measured through the biomarker heart rate variability (HRV).

The primary role of our nervous system is to ensure our survival and operates independently of conscious awareness, thus the term autonomic. The ventral vagus actively inhibits the sympathetic nervous system's influences on the heart and inhibits the

---

52   https://pdfs.semanticscholar.org/b96e/26723fe21b3139330e593a853f5cb25cb450. pdf?_ga=2.104787461.4668009 62.1581011040-580461231.1581011040

hypothalamic- pituitary adrenal (HPA) axis activity,[53,54] which may be thought of as the hormonal stress response.

Porges' work becomes important to our discussions in this book because he links ancient spiritual rituals and religious practices with the regulation of parasympathetic control mediated by vagal action, specifically the ventral vagal pathway, which is unique to mammals.[55] Porges concludes that ritual practices such chanting, prayer, somatic movements, and social engagement inherently balance the autonomic nervous system by bolstering the parasympathetic response.

> *"Embedded in religious and spiritual practices are manipulations of vagal pathways. Manipulation of vocalizations, breath, and posture engage and exercise specific vagal pathways that provide portals to compassion and health."*—**Stephen Porges (ibid).**

Kundalini yoga, a *Raj* yoga, is just one example of an ancient tradition that expresses Porges' emergent Polyvagal Theory and contains its major components.

---

53   Porges SW. The Polyvagal Theory: Phylogenetic substrates of a social nervous system. International Journal of Psychophysiology. 2001a;42:123–146. [PubMed] [Google Scholar]

54   The hypothalamus is a small endocrine structure in the brain that sits above the pituitary gland (master gland) and helps regulate the pituitary's release of hormones including those produced by the adrenal gland.

55   November 10, 2014. Stanford University Stephen Porges, PhD, Vagal Pathways: Portals to Compassion. https://youtu.be/LvdMleudqaA at 46:34

Ritual	Vagal Mechanism	Kundalini Yoga
Chants (vocalizations)	• Laryngeal nerves • Pharyngeal nerves • Respiration (long exhalation and deep abdominal inhalation enhance vagal 'brake')	Tuning-in Mantra Long-sustained syllables Naad yoga, primal vibrations
Meditation (breath)	• Respiration (long exhalation and deep abdominal inhalation enhance the vagal 'brake')	Pranayam Swara yoga (nostril)
Prayer (posture)	• Carotid baroreceptors (vagal contribution to blood pressure regulation)	Prayer pose Mudra (hand positions) Asana (postures)
Social Engagement	• Ventral vagus nerve • Slows heart rate	Yoga Class/Community Kirtan (communal chanting) Seva (selfless service)

Figure 9 Stephen W. Porges, The Physiology of Rituals,[56] used with permission.

_____

56   https://www.embodiedphilosophy.com/ancient-rituals-contemplative-practices-and-vagal-pathways/

Stephen Porges was an early pioneer quantifying HRV as a reliable index of vagal nerve activity; his research helped pioneer the connection among HRV, the parasympathetic nervous system, and vagal tonality.[57] Just as muscles can be toned with exercise, so too can the vagus nerve. An area of specific interest to Porges is the role of the parasympathetic nervous system control, mediated by the ventral vagus nerve, and compassion. He has found that stimulating the vagus nerve creates feelings of empathy and the instinct to nurture, and therefore calls the vagus nerve the "nerve of compassion."[58] This happens, in part, because the nerve stimulates receptor networks for oxytocin, a neurotransmitter that has been shown to increase trust and human bonding.

I happened upon the connection between parasympathetic activity and my own *Kundalini* yoga practice, specifically *pranayam* (yogic breathing) and chanting (mantra), when monitoring HRV. I noticed a consistent increase in parasympathetic activity and increased heart rhythm coherence during *pranayam* and chanting, quantifying the results using short-term HRV.

In the *Kundalini* yogic tradition,[59] the vagus nerve is referred to as "the central tuning string of the body." When the vagus nerve is "in tune," the parasympathetic and sympathetic systems are in harmony, and the heart enters into a coherent state or flow. As discussed in the earlier section, a coherent heart enables the rest of the body to resonate with the central tuning string, thus creating a harmonious vibration that can extend beyond the body and affect others nearby. Not only does the vagus nerve increase oxytocin, making us trust and want to bond, but affects the electromagnetic field or aura, making others trust and want to bond as well. Yogic exercises, such as breathing (*pranayam*) and postures, that focus on vagal nerve stimulation and parasympathetic rebalancing, highly effective for optimizing heart coherence, are discussed in Section Three.

---

57   Porges S. W. (2007). The polyvagal perspective. *Biological psychology, 74*(2), 116–143. doi:10.1016/j.biopsycho.2006.06.009

58   Porges, Stephen W. "The polyvagal perspective." *Biological Psychology* 74 (2) (2006): 116-43.

59   As taught by Yogi Bhajan

Heart-Brain Communication

J. Andrew Armour, a founding member of the International Neuro-cardiology Network and an emeritus professor at the University of Montreal, is an acclaimed leader and pioneer in the field of neuro-cardiology, the science at the intersection between the heart and the nervous system. In 1991, Armour introduced the term "heart brain" after conducting research that found the heart is a sensory organ with a unique, intrinsic nervous system independent of the brain. The heart does indeed have a *mind of its own*. Armour's findings continue to be expanded by researchers at the HeartMath® Institute. Figure 10 illustrates the bidirectional communication pathways of the vagus nerve going between the heart and brain.

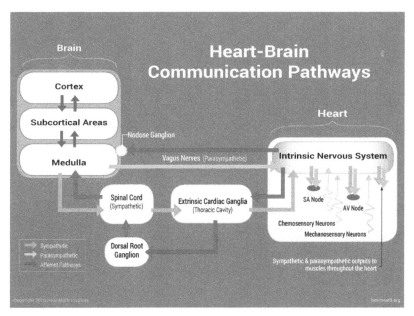

Figure 10 Credit: HeartMath® Neural pathways between heart and brain[60]The neural pathways between the heart and brain generate the variation of heart rate (HRV). The heart sends information to the brain based on emotional states and other inputs. Image credit: Courtesy of the HeartMath® Institute – www.heartmath.org.

---

60   https://www.heartmath.org/research/science-of-the-heart/heart

Through the heart-brain neural connections, conscious and unconscious negative thought patterns have immediate adverse effects on heart coherence. The psychological factors relating to heart coherence are discussed in the next section.

CHAPTER THREE

Heart Rhythm Coherence

"The goal of life is to make your heartbeat match the beat of the universe, to match your nature with Nature."

— **Joseph Campbell** (*Joseph Campbell Companion* 148)

If I were to choose one quote that sums up the essence of the term heart rhythm coherence, it would be this one by American mythologist Joseph Campbell. There's a submissive quality about it, for one must die, in a sense, in order to acquiesce to the rhythm of the universe. If I had to choose one word for heart rhythm coherence, it would be the *tao*, an ineffable ancient Chinese concept that includes the natural order of the universe.

Let me back up and review some basic terminology and concepts before unpacking these thoughts further, which will take the rest of the book and beyond.

The concept of coherence is the first term to become better acquainted with. Coherence can be defined as an orderly, logical, and harmonious interrelatedness among individual parts. The terms "coherence" and "coherent" come from the Latin *cohaerere: Co* means "together" and *haerere* means "to stick, adhere."

The Merriam-Webster dictionary defines coherence as:

♥ logically or aesthetically ordered or integrated: consistent

♥ having clarity or intelligibility: understandable

♥ having the quality of holding together or cohering: cohesive, coordinated

For the purposes of this book, I add one more attribute of coherence: an underlying creative intelligence or spirit that serves as the substrate for coherent behavior. For example, a book's author provides the intelligence behind the writing. One incoherent sentence can destabilize, as it were, an entire paragraph. While a single incoherent sentence or paragraph may not render a book meaningless, the more incoherent sentences or paragraphs there are, the less coherent the book will be as a whole. The author must consciously ensure the book is coherent.

But can we say the same of natural phenomena? A flock of birds may spontaneously converge and become a single coherent entity as the flock flies together in synchronized harmony, collectively appearing as one shape, then suddenly shifting and appearing as another, again and again, in a process known as *murmuration*. Witnessing such a spectacle is observing coherence in motion. There is a spatially significant relational component of the individual parts or birds to the whole. The flock moves as one entity, indicating some form of group intelligence is at work.

Nobel Prize-winning author John Steinbeck was mesmerized by the same phenomenon in schools of fish while on an expedition in the Sea of Cortez with biologist Ed Ricketts in the 1940s. He reflected that it was a fallacy to think of the school of fish that he observed as individual fish; rather, he perceived them to be "one unit" as they swam and turned in unison. (*Log of the Sea of Cortez* 243-244).

Many object that there is no intelligence behind coherence-based phenomena, pointing to the fact that inanimate objects, such as pendulum clocks, can spontaneously synchronize. Steven Strogatz, for example, concludes, "The sympathy of clocks taught us that the capacity for sync does not depend on intelligence, or life, or natural section. It springs from the deepest source of all: the law of mathematics and physics."[61] I agree with Strogatz's claim that mathematics underlies the cause of the synchronization of the clocks, however, I do not agree that mathematics is the terminal or "deepest source" for such behavior.

---

61   Steven Strogatz is a recognized leader in the field of chaos and complexity and the Schurman Professor of Applied Mathematics at Cornell University.

Such conclusions leave no room on the throne for other viewpoints (the reference to the throne relates back to Jung's quote in Chapter 4). Why stop short of attempting to unveil the mysteries behind the math, or at least acknowledge there may be more to mathematics than abstract numbers? Numbers and mathematics hold their own innate intelligence and mystery. Mathematical theories accept and acknowledge the use of infinity and irrational numbers, as well as paradoxes (like the idea that a mathematical *point* occupies no space). Mystery is an inextricable part of mathematics.

When we settle for understanding only the rules of physical phenomena, something is lost. As Rudolph Steiner said, "When we look out into this ocean and see the stars moving only according to mathematical lines, then we see the grave of the world's spiritual essence; for the divine Sophia, the successor of Isis is dead."[62] But it has never been entirely lost. The mechanistic view of the Enlightenment provoked the countermovement of Romanticism. To give one example: The 18th-century Romantic poet and artist William Blake saw mathematics divinely inspired, proclaiming that "God is a geometer." (Figure 11)

When I suggest that there is intelligence behind natural phenomena, I am not aligning myself with the "intelligent design" creationists who think the world was made exactly as it is now by an anthropomorphic deity. As Leroy Little Bear expresses in the foreword to *On Creativity*, written by theoretical physicist David Bohm, "What Blackfoot refer to as 'spirit' and energy waves are the same. All creation is spirit."[63] Little Bear's words capture the sense in which I use the words intelligence: as an energy at work that is constantly forming and reforming the world. Such concepts may allow us a common ground on which to move forward. It may be helpful to some if they substitute the words "infinite" or "paradox" for "intelligence" or "spirit."

---

62   https://wn.rsarchive.org/Lectures/GA202/English/MP1983/19201224p02.html
http://survivorbb.rapeutation.com/viewtopic.php?f=22&t=3485#p22043
63   1996, p. ix

Figure 11 Plate from Europe a Prophecy, copy K, in the collection of the Fitzwilliam Museum, Cambridge University. Image credit: Public Domain.[64]

---

64 https://commons.wikimedia.org/wiki/File:Europe_a_Prophecy_copy_K_ plate_01.jpg

Is it possible that coherence also holds some profound mystery? Evolutionary biologist and geneticist Dr. Mae-Wan Ho admits that "the idea of coherence is so foreign to most Western-trained scientists that there has been a lot of resistance to it from the mainstream."[65] But not all scientists resist the idea. David Bohm, for one, does not accept the Cartesian model of mind-body dualism. In *Wholeness and the Implicate Order,* he argues for "understanding the nature of reality in general and of consciousness in particular as a coherent whole, which is never static or complete but which is an unending process of movement and unfoldment." Bohm's theory is predicated on the notion that disparate multiplicities share an underlying unifying intelligence or consciousness.

Coherence theory is not limited to the behavior of physical objects like birds, fish, and pendulums. Coherence can be found in combinations of the physical and psychological, the psychological and spiritual, and on and on. Societies, religions, and solar systems all have varying degrees of coherence.[66] With a rudimentary understanding of how I am using the term coherence, we are now ready to turn our focus to heart coherence.

The Coherent Heart

In physics, coherence is a correlation between physical properties of a single waveform or multiple waveforms. The human heart generates a waveform that is either coherent or chaotic (or somewhere along that continuum) based on its electromagnetic generation, which I'll come back to. Harmony between our physical nature and Nature can be experienced through the rhythmic beating of the heart. Figure 12

---

65   *The Rainbow and the Worm: the Physics of Organisms* 116

66   Readers interested in the philosophy of coherence are encouraged to read Paul Thagard's *Coherence in Thought and Action,* in which he addresses such topics as knowledge, emotion, psychology, ethics, and politics. Thagard is a philosopher, cognitive scientist, and Distinguished Professor Emeritus of Philosophy at the University of Waterloo and a Fellow of the Royal Society of Canada, the Cognitive Science Society, and the Association for Psychological Science.

demonstrates the characteristic sine wave pattern of a healthy rhythm, a heart in harmony. The energy of the heart is focused and efficient. One can liken high heart coherence it to a laser beam, where energy is tightly focused in a single beam.

Low heart coherence has chaotic waveforms (see Figure 13), as do the dispersed waveforms of a 60-watt light bulb; both work, but not as efficiently as their coherent counterparts.

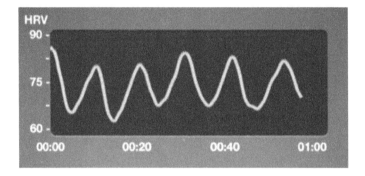

Figure 12 High heart coherence show as a sine wave.
Image credit: author using HeartMath® Inner Balance.

In contrast, the rhythm in Figure 13 is chaotic. The heart's energy is scattered, like the diffuse light of a 60-watt light bulb.

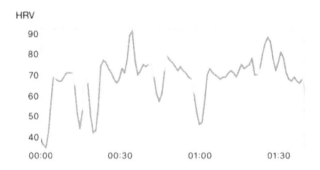

Figure 13 Chaotic pattern of low heart coherence.
Image credit: author using HeartMath® Inner Balance.

A coherent heart acts like a conductor in a symphony orchestra, setting the timing and rhythm for the performance of the entire body. When the conductor is in a coherent state, the performance is elevated, and the audience feels it emotionally. When the conductor is off kilter, so is the whole orchestra; the performance becomes incoherent. At best, it's lackluster and doesn't inspire the audience. If the incoherence is too great, the sound becomes discordant and unpleasant.

Our hearts are designed to fall into place—become coherent with—larger oscillating fields surrounding us. To match your heartbeat with the beat of the universe is the essence of heart coherence. When our own heart rhythm pattern synchronizes with the Earth's electromagnetic field we have fulfilled Joseph Campbell's directive, "The goal of life is to make your heartbeat match the beat of the universe, to match your nature with Nature[67]." Like the human heart, the Earth behaves like an electrical circuit and generates its own electromagnetic field. That's what you orient yourself to when you use a magnetic compass.

Between the surface of the Earth and the inner edge of the ionosphere, which is around 55 kilometers up, there is a gap or cavity. This cavity is continuously charged through lightning strikes happening around the world, approximately 50 every second. This charged energy oscillates between the Earth's surface and the ionosphere, creating a continuous frequency of around 7.83 Hz. This is known as the Schumann resonance, named after Winifred Schumann, who in 1952 correctly documented Tesla's theory of resonance effect.

"If you want to find the secrets of the universe, think in terms of energy, frequency and vibration" (Nikola Tesla).

Just as our hearts create their own unique frequency, the Earth creates its own frequency based on the electromagnetic field that the Earth generates between the north and south poles. Interestingly, the Schumann "constant" of 7.83 Hz appears to be shifting upward

---

67   https://www.jcf.org/works/quote/the-goal-of-life/

and exhibits huge spikes of more than 30 Hz. The ancient Indian Rishis knew the Schumann frequency as OM, the Sanskrit word "consciousness," or Ultimate Reality, the heartbeat of Mother Earth.

When your heart's electromagnetic field resonates or synchronizes with the Earth's electromagnetic field, we have successfully matched our beat to the beat of the Universe. Once heart coherence is achieved, it tends to stay in coherence until something knocks it off kilter.

Other factors, such as negative mental self-talk, chronic stress, anxiety, and depression can pull our heart rhythm patterns out of their normal sine wave pattern. Image if the Earth's tidal patterns looked more like the chaotic rhythms of an incoherent heart; hold this image until we explore tides and coherence further into the discussion. When the heart is in a state of incoherence, the body's energy is scattered—or worse, fighting itself. Energetically, low heart coherence creates chaos in our psyche-soma, and many of us wonder why we feel tired and depleted much of the time. This discordance may set the stage for disease.

When we're in sync with the stronger oscillating fields of the universe, we enter the zone of healing, high energy, and greater awareness. We have successfully "matched our heartbeat with the beat of the Universe." High heart coherence can even bring us into higher states of consciousness.

Heart Rate Variability: An Underutilized Biomarker

Heart coherence, or lack of it, is demonstrated in the spacing between heartbeats and their *rate of change*, as opposed to the morphology (shape) of each individual heartbeat. That is the domain of cardiologists. A healthy variation in heart rhythm occurs even when a person is at rest. A healthy heart is like a seasoned tennis player awaiting a powerful serve, who must be able to react instantaneously (or so it seems) to where the serve lands. This motion is purposeful and responsive, not erratic and directionless. Heart rate variability (HRV) provides a picture of the dynamic beat-to-beat changes in heart rate and how individual beats correlate to the overall heart rhythm. This is nothing short of a dynamic window into the ANS.

Although yet to become a standard practice, measurement of HRV has been in use for decades. It was first used in 1965 as fetal monitoring to assess the distress level of high-risk fetuses during labor. By the 1970s, HRV was being used to assess risk of death from heart disease.

There are many different ways that HRV is calculated, and most algorithms are proprietary. Understanding the mathematics involved is not necessary for the purposes of this book,[68] except to say that it is a measure of the variation in heartbeats against time.

Figure 14 pictures each individual heartbeat, each QRS complex, as individual birds on a wire. I use this example here so we don't confuse the heartbeat morphology itself (the QRS complex) with heart rhythm coherence. The distance between them is the time between beats.

The top of each bird's head (R) is where the measurement is typically taken to determine the relative distance between them.

Figure 14 QRS complexes (heartbeats) as birds on a wire. Image Credit: Author and AnnaliseArt[69].

---

68   Readers of a mathematical bent are encouraged to access these sources: Heart rate variability: Standards of measurement, physiological interpretation, and clinical use European Heart Journal (1996) 17, 354–381. Shaffer, F., et al. An Overview of Heart Rate Variability Metrics and Norms.

69   Image by <a href="https://pixabay.com/users/AnnaliseArt-7089643/?utm_source= link- attribution&utm_medium=referral&utm_campaign=image&utm_ content=4567921">Annalise Batista</a> from <a href="https://pixabay.com/?utm_source =link- attribution&utm_medium=referral&utm_campaign=image&utm _content=4567921">Pixabay</a>

A natural, normal heart rhythm is shown in Figure 15. Note that the intervals—the time between each QRS complex—are not exactly the same, as the normal heart speeds up when you breathe in and slows down as you breathe out.

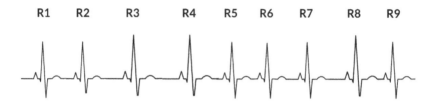

Figure 15 Normal variation in heart rate. Image Credit: Author

When you visit the doctor, the nurse usually checks your pulse for a minute. But a pulse of 60 beats per minute does not mean that your heart beats precisely once a second. A healthy heart pulsates to a dynamic rhythm that imperceptibly speeds up as you inhale and slows as you exhale. In other words, the rhythm is variable, and this variability indicates that the heart is responding correctly to how the rest of the body is functioning.

If your heart beat like a clock, once per second, this would indicate a highly *incoherent* heart. This may sound counterintuitive, but remember that variability is normal. A static heart rate of one beat per second indicates zero variability, as shown in Figure 16.

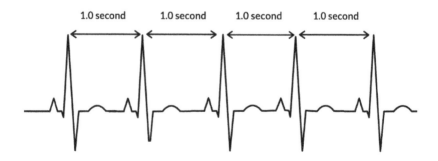

Figure 16 Zero variation in heart rate. Image credit: Author.

A low HRV score means that your heart is not as responsive as it could be and puts you at risk for many disease states. As stated before, low HRV is a predictor of all-cause mortality in heart disease patients and other clinical groups.[70] A higher HRV score usually means your heart is responding as it should to changing conditions, internal and external. Keep in mind that there is an optimal range for HRV, and higher doesn't necessarily mean better, as I attempted to articulate in the Goldilocks metaphor earlier.

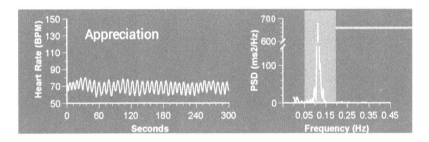

Figure 17 Two representations of HRV. Image credit: the HeartMath® Institute – www.heartmath.org.

The graph above represents waveform HRV data where heart rate is plotted against time. In this example, it shows what the rhythm of a heart in a highly coherent state looks like when plotted against time. It does not show the individual QRS complexes, just the rhythm of the beat-to-beat changes against time. The result is a smooth sine waveform: the hallmark of a coherent heart.

The graph on the right uses the same data mathematically converted to frequency (Hz),[71] providing what is called a frequency power spectrum display. The hallmark of a coherent heart on such a graph is that the data is concentrated around the 0.1 Hz mark for the majority of people.

---

70   Fang SC, Wu YL, Tsai PS. Heart Rate Variability and Risk of All-Cause Death and Cardiovascular Events in Patients With Cardiovascular Disease: A Meta-Analysis of Cohort Studies [published correction appears in Biol Res Nurs. 2020 Feb 28;:109980042 0909152]. *Biol Res Nurs.* 2020;22(1):45-56. doi:10.1177/1099800419877442

71   Using the Fast Fourier transform algorithm.

Figure 18 provides another representation of the *just right* level of HRV clustering around the 0.1Hz mark.

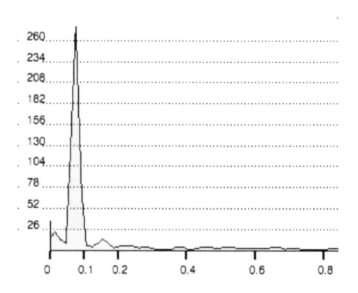

Figure 18 The "just right" point of heart coherence on a power spectrum frequency graph. Image credit: Author using HeartMath® Desktop.

"Just right" HRV (optimal HRV) will show a spike between 0.04 and 0.15 Hz, indicating that the sympathetic and parasympathetic systems are in dynamic balance. If the spike is lower than 0.04 Hz, it indicates that the sympathetic nervous system is dominating. If it is above 0.15 Hz, the parasympathetic system is dominating.

Low Coherence

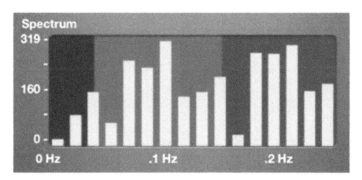

High Coherence

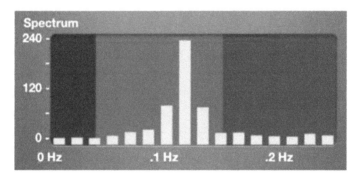

Figure 19 Power spectrum displays of low and high coherence. Image credit: Author using HeartMath® Inner Balance iPhone app.

As one would expect, the energy of the incoherent heart (top graph) is dispersed rather than clustered around the 0.1 Hz mark. In this case, parasympathetic activity is higher than sympathetic. This indicates a relaxed state, but not a coherent state. The heart is not working as efficiently as it could, even though there is high parasympathetic activity. Keep in mind, relaxation does not equal coherence. Let's go a little deeper to see why.

A Dynamic Window into the
Autonomic Nervous System

Several studies have shown that low HRV is an independent predictor of sudden cardiac death.[72] In *Human Heart, Cosmic Heart: A Doctor's Quest to Understand, Treat, and Prevent Cardiovascular Disease*, Dr. Thomas Cowan stresses the importance of parasympathetic activity in the role of heart disease. He concludes, "In the vast majority of [heart disease] cases, the pathology proceeds because of decreased tonic activity of the parasympathetic nervous system. Then there is an increase in sympathetic nervous system activity [.   ]."[73] If Cowan's assertion is correct, self-regulation of the ANS has an impact on heart pathology and, according to Buckberg, also the *form* of the heart. Cowan is not alone in his convictions regarding ANS health and the implications for heart disease.

Short-term HRV home monitoring[74] (HRV biofeedback) is non-invasive and inexpensive way to monitor HRV and self-regulate in order to counteract the harmful effects of chronic stress, anxiety, and depression. It can help you learn how to raise your heart coherence into the *just right* zone. Figure 19 shows an example from one monitoring application where the bulk of activity lies between 0.05-0.15 Hz, the *just right* zone.

---

72   Heikki V Huikur, et al. *Journal of the American College of Cardiology* 34 (7) December 1999: 1878–1883
73   (Cowan MD, 2016, pp. 57-58)
74   As opposed to 24-Hour Holter ECG monitoring, which was designed to be used for diagnostic purposes by clinicians.

Spectrum

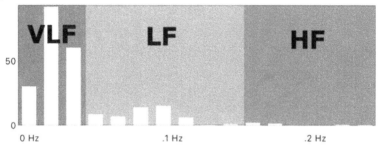

Figure 20 Biofeedback using HeartMath® Inner Balance.
VLF = very low frequency, LF = low frequency, HF = high
frequency. Image credit: Author using HeartMath® Inner Balance.

The bars on the left show that the ANS is out of balance; the sympathetic nervous system is dominating. The subject is in some level of fight-or-flight mode, resulting in low HRV and low heart coherence.

Spectrum

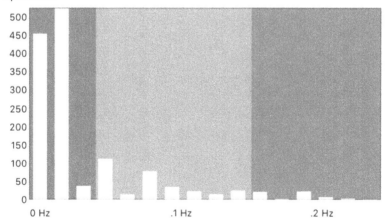

Figure 21 Sympathetic nervous system dominating in VLF,
using HeartMath® Inner Balance. Image credit: author.

Again in Figure 21, most of the ANS activity is far to the left in the sympathetic portion, leaving the parasympathetic branch impaired. The person is in fight-or-flight mode. For many people, this is their default position and puts them at risk of stress-induced diseases.

Figure 22 represents the other end of the spectrum, a state of overrelaxation where parasympathetic activity is the dominant pattern. HRV is very high, yet chaotic, yielding low heart coherence. The coherence ratio gauge is 100% in the red zone. This is not a desirable long- term pattern either (although most people aren't in a relaxed state for long periods).

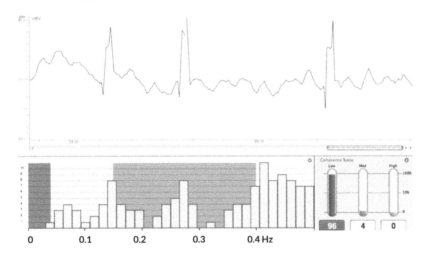

Figure 22 Parasympathetic activity dominating. Image credit: Author using emWave® HeartMath® Desktop software.

Although the optimal HRV score for high heart coherence centers around 0.1 Hz (using HeartMath® technologies) for most people, HRV itself *is variable,* which ultimately creates long-term patterns reflecting systemwide order. The tidal image coming up later illustrates this point beautifully. Optimized coherence settling around the 01. Hz mark is rarely sustained. Most people are typically in lower states of heart rhythm coherence during their day-to-day activities and unmanaged fluctuating emotional states. Figure 23 shows how a healthy and balanced ANS will have a dynamic flow between sympathetic and parasympathetic systems.

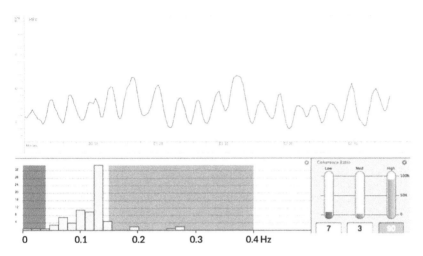

Figure 23 Predominantly balanced HRV with most activity occurring around the 0.1 mark. Image credit: Author using emWave® HeartMath® Desktop.

There is no pill to correct low HRV.[75] It is imperative that people take responsibility to understand that while depression leads to disease states including heart attacks, the mainstream "cure" for depression, anti-depressant medication, may be putting you further at risk of future health problems.

---

75 Implantable vagus nerve stimulators have been used to improve major depression in patients. While readers are encouraged to consult their health care providers, it is important to note that there is no substitute for emotional self-regulation, which can be layered onto any existing treatment or therapy.

Which Came First: the Chicken or the Egg?

The relationship between depression and low HRV has long been established in mainstream medical literature[76, 77, 78]. What is less clear is the relationship among antidepressant medications, heart attacks (and other stress-induced illnesses), and heart rate variability. Researchers Dr. C. O'Regan, et al., posed the following question in their research study[79]: "Heart rate variability (HRV) is known to be reduced in depression; however, is unclear whether this is a conse-quence of the disorder or due to antidepressant medication."[80] Their research suggests that reductions in HRV observed among depressed older adults, those most at risk for heart disease, are driven by the effects of antidepressant medications (ibid). It should be noted that there are conflicting studies and conclusions regarding the relation-ship among depression, anxiety, HRV, medications, and probability of future heart attacks and other stress-related diseases.

Researchers at the Center for Compassion and Altruism Research and Education at Stanford University have concluded that "HRV is an important physiological marker for overall health, and the

---

76   Carney RM, Freedland KE, Veith RC. Depression, the autonomic nervous system, and coronary heart disease. *Psychosom Med*. 2005;67 Suppl 1:S29-S33. doi:10.1097/01. psy.0000162254.61556.d5

77   Chalmers JA, Quintana DS, Abbott MJ, Kemp AH. Anxiety Disorders are Associated with Reduced Heart Rate Variability: A Meta-Analysis. *Front Psychiatry*. 2014;5:80. Published 2014 Jul 11. doi:10.3389/fpsyt.2014.00080

78   Hu, M. X., Penninx, B., de Geus, E., Lamers, F., Kuan, D. C., Wright, A., Marsland, A. L., Muldoon, M. F., Manuck, S. B., & Gianaros, P. J. (2018). Associations of immuno-metabolic risk factors with symptoms of depression and anxiety: The role of cardiac vagal activity. *Brain, behavior, and immunity, 73*, 493–503. https://doi.org/10.1016/j. bbi.2018.06.013

79   O'Regan, C., Kenny, R. A., Cronin, H., Finucane, C., & Kearney, P. M. (2015). Antidepressants strongly influence the relationship between depression and heart rate variability: findings from The Irish Longitudinal Study on Ageing (TILDA). *Psychological medicine, 45*(3), 623–636. https://doi.org/10.1017/S0033291714001767

80   O'Regan, C., Kenny, R. A., Cronin, H., Finucane, C., & Kearney, P. M. (2015). Antidepressants strongly influence the relationship between depression and heart rate variability: findings from The Irish Longitudinal Study on Ageing (TILDA). *Psychological medicine, 45*(3), 623–636. https://doi.org/10.1017/S0033291714001767

body-mind connection."[81] HRV monitoring has the potential to assuage heart problems resulting from chronic stress by elevating heart coherence as well as helping people self-regulate their emotional states.

As this book supports making room on the throne for other approaches, it is essential to consider the role of experiential-based cause and effect of optimizing HRV. After all, optimal HRV is one thing that the researchers seem to agree on when it comes to health and well-being. HRV biofeedback has significant potential for self-regulating the stress response, resulting in feelings of greater calm, less anxiety, less depression, greater compassion, and better sleep. You don't need a research study to determine how your emotional states affect your HRV. I have found no downside to emotional self-regulation while monitoring HRV, in myself or in my clients. The goal is to optimize your HRV; how you get there is less important. The following experiential exercise is one that I found helpful in regulation my own HRV, ultimately, heart coherence.

EXPERIENTIAL PRACTICE

Heartbeat Awareness Meditation[82]

The Heartbeat Awareness Meditation comes from the *Kundalini* yoga tradition. It is an excellent beginner's meditation and is nonstrenuous. This meditation gives you a pragmatic way to shift mental focus to your heart center by following the pulse. By placing your four fingertips on the wrist and feeling your pulse you create a focal point that draws your awareness to it.

---

81 Kirby, 2017
82 As taught by Harbhajan Singh Khalsa (Yogi Bhajan).

Tune-in[83] (Vocalization)

Chant three times: *Ong Namo Guru Dev Namo*

Posture
Sit either on the floor in easy pose (cross-legged) or in a chair. Ensure that your spine is straight. Tuck you chin in slightly into "neck-lock" (*jalandhar bandh*).

Hand Position (Mudra)
With four fingers of your right hand, feel for your pulse at your left wrist. Press gently and see if you can feel your pulse at each fingertip.

Vocalization (Mantra)
Silent vibration. With each beat of your heart (lub-dub), mentally (silently) vibrate *SAT NAM*[84].

Eye Position (Dhrist)
Eyes are closed and focused at the third eye point (between the eyebrows).

Breath Pattern (Pranayam)
Allow the breath to flow naturally.

Visualization
Still the mind and focus on the breath, minimizing emotional interference. When the mind wanders, simply notice and come back to your breath.

Time
Continue for 11 minutes or up to 31 minutes (it takes 11 minutes to begin to affect the ANS).

---

83 Tuning In: Translation: I bow to the infinite teacher within, and open myself to the infinite source of wisdom, healing, and creativity within me. Before beginning any *Kundalini* yoga practice, "tune-in" with the Adi Mantra, which sets an intention to connect with your infinite Self within. This also helps to set practice time apart from your normal daily routine. Tuning-in is a call to your higher Self, the healer within, and aligns you with Infinite source. Set an intention for healing your stress and anxiety as you connect with your inner Heart's Wisdom.

84 Sat Nam translates to "truth is my identity."

Contraindication

If you begin to feel dizzy, stop the exercise.

Optional HRV Biofeedback

If you have an HRV biofeedback device, you may choose to use it during meditation. For many people, until they learn how to meditate, HRV biofeedback may be too distracting as there can be a tendency to check in and see how you're doing.

Note: Different meditations affect people differently. By finding a meditation that resonates with you, you can begin to experience improved heart coherence.

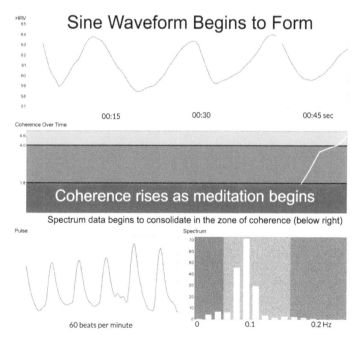

Figure 24 HRV Biofeedback session during Heartbeat Awareness Meditation, Image credit: Author using HeartMath® Inner Balance app.

Note: Every person will experience his or her own level of coherence while practicing this or any meditation. Factors include overall ANS functionality, mental state, and the breath.

Depth Psychology
and the Heart

*"To know the strong masculine principle, yet abide
by the gentle female principle, is like being the
valley of the world where all rivers will flow into."*

— the I Ching

CHAPTER FOUR

Depth Psychology

"The psyche is the starting point of all human experience, and all the knowledge we have gained eventually leads back to it. It is not only the object of its science, but the subject also."

– Carl G. Jung[85]

In this book, I use the word "psyche" in the Jungian sense of the word, which is both multifaceted and somewhat nebulous. "Psyche" includes conscious and unconscious awareness, both personal and collective, whose boundaries are unclear. The unconscious is also called the "deep" psyche; this is the concern of depth psychology.

Carl G. Jung was a scientist, a psychiatrist and psychotherapist who practiced in Switzerland during the first half of the 20th century. A protégé of Sigmund Freud, Jung was a pioneer in his understanding of the important relationship between the conscious and unconscious psyche. Ultimately, Jung and Freud had a parting of ways due to differing opinions on central theories. The traumatic split with Freud plunged Jung into a kind of breakdown, during which he plumbed the depths of his own unconscious. Out of this experience he ultimately forged revolutionary theories, including those of the collective unconscious and the individuation process as a path to wholeness.

Jung was first and foremost a Western medical doctor and advocate of modern medicine. He believed that Western science was stronger when it maintained its inherent boundaries, which rely on reproducible cause and effect. Yet he warned that:

---

85   "The Psychological Factors in Human Behavior" (*CW* 8 par 261).

Science is not indeed a perfect instrument, but it is a superb and invaluable tool that works harm only when it is taken as an end in itself. Science must serve; it errs when it usurps the throne. It must be ready to serve all branches, for each, because of its insufficiency, has need of support from the others. Science is the tool of the Western mind, and with it one can open more doors than with bare hands. It is part and parcel of our understanding, and it obscures our insight only when it claims that the understanding it conveys is the only kind there is.[86]

For science to deny that which lies outside its boundaries is an error. When Western science denies the validity of other healing modalities and "usurps the throne," people suffer both physically and psychologically.

Jung and Archetypes

Jung's theory of the collective unconscious holds that all humans are linked at the deepest level of the psyche. This shared field manifests in our awareness as archetypal images.

Archetypes are concepts universal to all humans—for example, the archetype of Mother, which all humans recognize. Archetypes cannot be directly observed; however, they give rise to images that come into our awareness and trigger reverberations within us as we recognize their significance.

Jung began to suspect the presence of the collective unconscious as he worked with patients who would dream of images from cultures far away in time and space—cultures of which they had no conscious knowledge. Jung found that these dream images also offered rich wisdom from the deep psyche, wisdom not otherwise available to the individual. Symbols, whether in architecture, poetry, or dreams, contain layer upon layer of meaning. Depending on what level the

---

86   Alchemical Studies

seeker has attained on his or her spiritual path or where one is in the process of individuation, symbols speak at the level most suitable to the individual. Jung developed techniques that allow individuals to work with dream images and unveil their personal meaning.

Jung believed that mythological figures and archetypal images provide us with a mechanism to resolve our own complexes. Complexes are both conscious and unconscious. They are emotionally charged representations of some kind of internal conflict, usually rooted in a painful experience. Jung understood that throughout the history of humankind, complexes were expressed through mythological symbols and images, such as the pantheon of Greek gods (Zeus represents our Father issues, for instance). Resolving these conflicts frees us from their energy and returns us to wholeness.

Religions offer us ways of working with these energies through rich imagery and rituals, such as confession and atonement. As people have turned away from religion to science, these rituals have lost their power for many. Yet, complexes remain. Without an external outlet, they often surface as symptoms, even outright illnesses. "The gods have become diseases; Zeus no longer rules Olympus but the solar plexus, and creates specimens for the physician's consulting room," Jung said.[87] Instead of confessing to a priest, we now confess to a doctor—often to be told "it's all in your head" when the lab or X-ray machine cannot find a cause for our symptoms.

The scientific attitude has also estranged us from imagination, telling us that art, stories, our fantasies are not "real." In today's schools, STEM (science, technology, engineering, and math) takes precedence while the arts are neglected or underfunded. When individuals lose their faculty of imagination, we become estranged from our souls. Meaning drains from our lives.

This soulless life becomes the seed bed for disease.

To counter this attitude, Jung taught that one can derive meaning in life by progressing on the path of individuation, the arduous journey

---

87 *Secret of the Golden Flower* 113

of becoming acquainted with one's own uniqueness. The process of individuation requires exploration beyond the façade of the persona (the mask that one shows the world) and the willful ego to find the inner Self and the true, individual personality. As people individuate, they expand consciousness. The process also requires the person to resolve complexes, to reconcile internal conflicts, which Jung found can often be done through the use of symbols.[88]

Jung believed that the Self, which he defined as the archetype of wholeness, is the central organizing principle within the psyche. Yet the Self is often obscured by the ego, our conscious and self-protective idea of who we are supposed to be. The realignment of Self and ego is a process that moves one toward "psychological coherence," or individuation. In a fully individuated person, the ego surrenders to the higher authority of the Self.

As part of the individuation process, unconscious psychic contents are gradually brought into conscious awareness for psychological processing. Conscious awareness is associated with the light of day, the sun, and masculine archetypal energies, whereas the unconscious is related to the feminine principles of the moon, darkness, and that which lies veiled. In one of Jung's lectures, he used the symbol of the sine wave to describe the process of individuation[89]. The process follows a serpentine path that undulates between conscious and unconscious awareness. Unconscious material comes to the surface in dreams, allowing the conscious mind access.

To refuse the work of individuation leads to a life that lacks deep meaning. Meaning comes from within; when it is sought externally (through money, for example), disappointment is unavoidable. The more we try to find meaning outside of ourselves, the more it eludes us—as can be seen in successful actors and sports stars who, despite fame and money, often turn to drugs and alcohol to numb their inner pain.

---

88 MDR 344
89 Jung, C. G. *Visions: Notes of the Seminar Given in 1930-1934.* Lecture VIII, June 29, 1932.

Lack of meaning in one's life also sows the seeds of disease. Complexes can be thought of as trapped psychic energy. The work of individuation helps free this energy. If it is not released, it will manifest eventually as physical discomfort.

Archetypal Heart Coherence

The post-Jungian psychologist James Hillman, who founded the school of Archetypal Psychology, viewed disease as an opportunity for expanding consciousness: "Each organ has a potential spark of consciousness, and afflictions release this consciousness."[90] Disease, including addictions and depression, serves as a somatic warning alarm, bringing attention to the need for wholeness and the recovery of the lost soul.

Hillman believed that the soul incarnates with a preformed "blueprint," and that part of the meaning of life is to find one's true calling, to discover what the blueprint for your life is and apply it. He called this his "acorn theory." Just as the destiny of the acorn is to become an oak tree, we have a destiny that is ours to discover and fulfill.

Hillman's acorn theory echoes Plato's "Myth of Er," which states that the soul incarnates with a specific destiny. However, prior to birth the soul drinks from the river of Lethe to forget this destiny. Like Jung, Hillman believed that the task for each individual is to discover and fulfill one's unique destiny, to individuate—to find what I call psychological coherence. Along with engaging with images, this task can be accomplished by working within the imaginal realm, the psychological "betwixt and between" state that links reality as we know it and the unconscious psyche.

Hillman credits Islamic scholar Henry Corbin[91] with setting forth the primary principle of the *imaginal heart,* a concept that helped shift the focus of depth psychology to imagination, culture,

---

90   Hillman, James. *Blue Fire* 162
91   Henry Corbin (1903-1978) scholar of Islamic mysticism, professor of Islam and Islamic Philosophy at Sorbonne in Paris and University of Tehran. Interested readers are directed to *Alone with the Alone: Creative Imagination in the Sufism of Ibn 'Arabi.*

and the archetypal qualities of psyche. Corbin recognized the need to reintroduce the lost concept of soul back into Western culture. His contribution was to translate and explicate the writings of Ibn 'Arabi and other Islamic mystics. Hillman's *The Thought of the Heart and the Soul of the World* relies heavily on Corbin's work. However, Corbin's work is spiritually based; he believed that wholeness lies not in holding the tension of opposites but in transcending the dark forces[92] of the lower soul (*nafs* in the Islamic tradition), of which the battlefield is the human heart.

From Hillman's perspective, the *mundus imaginalis* does not carry spiritual overtones; rather, it remains within the boundaries, however mercurial, of a psychology of soul. Depth psychologist Robert Sardello criticized Hillman for this, saying, "Depth psychology is unable to distinguish the realm of the unconscious and the realm of the super-conscious. Hillman's interpretation of the *Mundus Imaginalis* is a misinterpretation." (qtd. in *Green Man* xiii) Corbin himself cautioned, "If this term [imaginal] is used to apply to anything other than *mundus imaginalis* and the imaginal Forms as they are located in the schema of the worlds [homologues, seeds, or cascading schema] which necessitate them and legitimize them." (*Spiritual Body* xviii)

Corbin adopted Islamic symbolism when he equated the *mundus imaginalis* with the "eighth climate," a world or plane between the spiritual and material accessed through active Imagination (Corbin's capitalization). He wrote, "Between the world of pure spiritual Lights . . . and the sensory universe, at the boundary of the ninth Sphere (the Sphere of Spheres) there opens a *mundus imaginalis* which is a concrete spiritual world of archetype-Figures, apparitional Forms, Angels of species and of individuals . . ." (*Man of Light* 42) The imaginal realm straddles the sensible reality that humans live in and the inexpressible spiritual world. Corbin considered the *mundus imaginalis* (*'alam a mithal*) to be the realm of the archetypes or a place "outside" of place, the land of No-where).

---

92 Corbin's perspective of the need to transcend the dark rather than synthesize it is consistent with Wisdom traditions, including *Kundalini* yoga which translates the term "guru" as moving from darkness to light.

Corbin explained that there are three realms: the realm of the physical, the realm of the divine, and in between them, what he called the imaginal realm: the "betwixt and between" realm. Christianity expresses a similar idea with Jesus, who is poised between God and Man and has elements of both and so serves as a bridge for humans to access the divine. To Jung and Hillman, the imaginal realm is the place where the soul and the body can talk to each other.

Corbin contended that "masters of mythical vision have seen the interworld as something contiguous to the spiritual world, receiving light from it [. . .] as high windows allow rays of light to enter a house." (*Spiritual Body* 146) The *imaginal* realm is where the poets and literary masters dwell, engaging and playing in and with the imaginal world.

The Serpentine Sine Wave to Individuation

The individuation process is a method of making unconscious contents conscious, in part through the reconciliation of internal opposites. This usually involves dealing with our complexes, for when there is a weighty charge or emotion around an archetypal image, it is often a sign that a complex is in play. Complexes can be thought of as strong emotions all tangled up in a particular memory or experience, often a traumatic one. When a person is reminded of the event, those strong emotions resurface; conversely, when the person experiences a similar emotion for another reason, he or she may be reminded of the trauma—as happens in flashbacks for people suffering from posttraumatic stress disorder. Often these complexes become tied to a particular archetype, so another way to describe a complex is the energy that surrounds a sensitized archetypal core.

The rhythmic process of dipping into the unconscious psyche followed by an encounter with an archetype may generate images that rise up into the conscious mind. During the Jung's "Visions" seminar, he and his participants suggested that conscious awareness is analogous to masculine, or *yang,* consciousness,[93] and feminine

---

93   from the *Tao Te Ching* and *Yang-Yin* philosophy.

yin energy is the terrain of the unconscious psyche (see Figure 25. Jung and his participants established that the individuation process followed a snake-like progression.

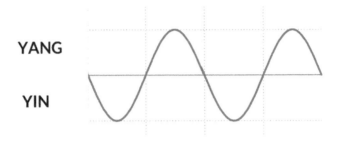

Figure 25 Sine wave concept showing YIN below the baseline and YANG above the baseline. Image credit: Author.

Jung's individuation process requires a descent into unconscious terrain of *yin*, which harbors the rich field on archetypes. During the "Visions" seminar, Jung associated the unconscious psyche with feminine archetypal images such as the Great Mother, water, ocean, earth, and chthonic or underworld realms (Visions, 1997, p. 711). The dark unchartered woods serve as another metaphor for delving into the unconscious psyche, the mythical feminine unknown, where the dreamer or visioner encounters a challenge or situation. As the psychic contents rise up to the threshold of consciousness, the images may pass into the conscious psyche, where the rational mind can begin to process the *prima materia*. It does so by collecting, categorizing, amplifying, and making associations with the newly emerging archetypal images. In the "light of day," so to speak, the *yang* masculine energy attempts to analyze and rationalize the dream or vision contents via *logos* of rational analysis. At times when the portal to the archetypal realm is open, a person may have instantaneous knowing, or *gnosis*, as the intuition knowing what is being transmitted without analysis. An example of such direct knowing will be given in the Appendix titled "Roland's Vision." The essential point is that Roland "sees" the letter "C" awakening from surgery and instantly understands his soul's urgent cry to open his heart to compassion.

Such symbolic images are alchemical gold and bring to light submerged psychic contents for processing, either by oneself or a competent professional. Dream fragments are just that, bits and pieces of wisdom delivered from the unconscious to the conscious psyche in symbolic language, which speaks to the intuitive feminine right brain rather than logical masculine left brain. Symbols have the unique ability to unite unconscious and conscious thought.

Once the archetypal images are initially processed, understood to a first level, and then integrated, a person is ready to dip back down into the unconscious realm to unearth new and fresh material. Similar to the waxing and waning moon, the eternal ebb and flow of the tides, the sun's day and night journey, the process of individuation requires immersion into the unconscious and reemergence into conscious awareness as an ongoing, eternal process. Consider a whale, for example, that takes a deep breath, symbolic of the *yang* conscious psyche, and then submerges into deep water of *yin*. The nutrients are *under* the water, not on the surface or air above.

Similarly, our psychic nutrients in the form of archetypal images, are in the *yin* portion of psyche, and we "come up for air" in order to process what we have involuntarily received.

This rhythmic sinusoidal process necessitates entering into the feminine and masculine (unconscious and conscious) portions of psyche in right proportion.[94] If we stay too long in the unconscious feminine/*yin*, there is a risk of being overtaken and overwhelmed by the experience. Jung experienced this phenomenon during his early days and captured the images in what is now known as *The Red Book: Liber Novus*. The multitude of symbols provided the *prima materia* for his life's work. However, at times Jung was at risk of being engulfed by the unconscious; the material simply could not be processed quickly enough by the conscious *yang* mind. Jung's early journey toward individuation provides an example of a highly incoherent path where

---

94   The term "right proportion" is being used here in conjunction with the Rainmaker story (retold at the end of this section) where the *tao* keeps things in harmonious balance.

the rhythmic flow remained in the unconscious for disproportionate periods of time.

On the other hand, if one spends little time engaged with the unconscious, for example, by dismissing dream images as meaningless or not doing sufficient work in capturing emerging images, then the conscious psyche has no new material to process, and one does not further along on the individuation process. Such is the case for much of modern society. The masculine conscious/*yang* portion of psyche dominates the dance. Using Jung's sine wave graph in Figure 25, one can imagine most of the energy settling above the dotted line. From an HRV standpoint, this is analogous to excessive sympathetic activity and low heart coherence.

Another interesting point that was raised in the June 1 1932, seminar is one of the evolution of the individuation process and its relation to time. As new psychic contents rise to the brink of consciousness and are successfully processed and integrated, the person moves further toward a completed individuation process, or "absolute center." Insights that are realized and integrated by a person, whether done privately or with an analyst/healer, provide a path to the expansion of one's conscious awareness. In other words, the person evolving and progressing on the path of individuation does not return to the same place or baseline where she/he started; rather, the path is spiral in nature, bringing one into higher awareness based on the psychic contents successfully integrated into his/her consciousness. This concept was modeled in Jung's seminar where a sine wave was drawn into the notes symbolizing the progression of the individuation process. Jung recognized the spiral nature of the individuation process as its movement toward completion when he said, "The idea, I should say, would be a sort of oscillating peripheral movement approaching a center, and the end of the growth would always be closer to the absolute center than the beginning." (Jung, Visions, 1997, p. 714) To this, participant Mr. Allemann suggested, "The wavy line is the spiral" (715) to which Jung countered "Yes, it is most probably a spiral, which is the fundamental law in the growth of a plant [. . .]" (715), and as we have seen, the spiral is the universal path of growth.

Thus, the individuation process follows the universal process of growth. Psyche *is* nature. The archetypal phallic shaped image from *Visions: Notes of the Seminar Given in 1930-1934 by C. G. Jung* (page 715) represents the universal symbol of creation, the cosmogonic myth and is generative similar to the Orphic World Egg, also referred to as the golden womb, golden fetus, and is a creation mytheme that is integral to civilizations since time immemorial, from ancient Egypt, Chinese, Finland, Greece, the Vedic traditions and well beyond.

Figure 26 World egg. Image credit: Creative Commons.

The primary inner conflict that needs reconciliation, the one most pertinent to heart rhythm coherence, is the conflict between our inner masculine and feminine aspects. Jung used the terms *animus* and *anima* (Latin for "soul") to represent the masculine and feminine archetypal forces within. These forces often speak to us in dreams. Jung considered them the gateway to the unconscious. Emma Jung, wife of C. G. Jung, recognized this about psychological masculine and feminine dynamics: "[. . .] life is founded on the harmonious interplay of masculine and feminine forces, within the individual human being as well as without. Bringing these opposites into union is one of the most important tasks of present-day psychotherapy" (Emma Jung, 1955).

Individuation requires psychological restoration of the feminine principle within the human psyche in both men and women by healing the internal *anima-animus* dynamic. Doing so results in an "inner marriage," or *coniunctionis*, a resolution of internal opposites. The method uses archetypal imagination and active engagement with images as perceived through the heart.

Temple of the Heart

> *"The Temple must be first built in the heart."*
> —**Henry Corbin** (*Temple and Contemplation* 343)

The archetypal significance of the temple archetype traverses millennia, place, and culture—from the Mesopotamian temple of Inanna at Uruk to the ancient Greek Temple of Venus to the Hagia Sophia (Temple of the Holy Wisdom) and to the Star (Sirius) of the Maltese Temples. The divine Feminine has been at the center of the temple archetype and serves as a guiding star for the spiritual heart that dwells within.

When we think of ancient temples, stones may be a first image that comes to mind. For us to enter the temple archetype, I will pick up the temple image from Jung's heart attack vision series and then bring it into the realm of the temple within the imaginal heart. The following excerpt is from Jung's *Memories, Dreams, Reflections,* where he recounts his approach to a stone temple during his near-death heart attack experience.

"A short distance away I saw in space a tremendous dark block of stone, like a meteorite. It was about the size of my house, or even bigger." (*Memories, Dreams, Reflections* 290) Although an entire study could be dedicated to Jung's archetypal associations with stones, I mention a few key examples here. As a child, the large square blocks of stone in an old garden wall fascinated Jung, and he often sat upon them. Jung recalls his unique association with stones in *Memories, Dreams, Reflections* when, as a child, he mused, "'Am I the one sitting on the stone and it is underneath?'" Jung unknowingly engages in active imagination with the stone when the stone responds, "Or am I the stone on which *he* is sitting?" (20) From his early days, Jung views stones as more than inert objects, possessing something hidden or secret deep within them.

As a schoolboy, Jung carved the top of his ruler into a manikin, which he named Philemon, and supplied him with a painted stone, delineated into upper and lower halves. This image presages Jung's later theory of conscious and unconscious aspects of the human psyche. Bair quotes Jung from the unpublished and uncirculated document *Protocols:* "Later, when I read Greek mythology, I discovered when Zeus was troubled in love he would sit down on a stone [. . .]. In my case it was not a question of troubled love, but of who 'I' really was." (qtd. in *Jung: A Biography* 660) Jung's identity, his Self, was metaphorically hidden in the stone, and an alchemical process of individuation was required to release his captive Self.

Jung's vision of the stone, as an image of his sacred Self, further opens in the following sequence: "An entrance led into a small antechamber. To the right of the entrance, a black Hindu sat silently in lotus posture upon a stone bench. He wore a white gown, and I know that he expected me." (*Memories, Dreams, Reflections* 290)

Mysterium Coniunctionis, a post-heart-attack work of Jung's, provides significant insight to his perspective on stone symbolism, which factors largely into his alchemical perspectives.

Jung's alchemical studies were derived, in part, from the works of Gerhard Dorn, a 16th-century alchemist. In "The Conjunction," Jung wrote, "Dorn's *caelum*, which corresponded to the stone, was on the one hand a liquid [blue] that could be poured out of a bottle and on the other the Microcosm itself. For the psychologist it is the self—man as he is, and the indescribable and superempirical totality of that same man." (*CW* 14:765) In Jung's same essay published in *Mysterium Coniunctionis*, Jung describes *caelum* as a heavenly substance containing all distinct forms and simultaneously the ultimate universal form; it symbolizes a prefiguration of the soul. Jung also associates *caelum* with the blue center of Eastern mandalas. (*CW* 14:757) The *caelum* and its function in alchemy, as inviting as they are, provide an avenue for further study. Jung further contended in the same essay, "Man himself is partly empirical, partly transcendental; he too is a λίθος ού λίθος" [stone that is no stone]. A "stone that is not stone" reflects Jung's earlier experience with active imagination (also called trancing), where *he* (Jung) is sitting on *me* (stone). From this perspective, consciousness lies within the stone. Corbin uses the image of the pearl held within the black stone as the archetypal equivalent of a "stone that is not stone." The human parallel implies that consciousness lies within the human body and that the human heart is more than a blood pump. Like the pearl encased in stone, the heart is at the center of consciousness, which emanates from the divine.

In Jung's vision, the meditating yogi sits upon a lotus positioned on a stone. With contemplation (meditation), the spiritual seeker purifies his or her heart, thereby concentrating the power of the heart (*himma*) to reflect the divine. From this concentrated power of the heart, the temple emerges—the inside turns outward. Tom Cheetham, Henry Corbin scholar, explores this Islamic mystical concept in detail in his book *The World Turned Inside Out*. Jung's imagination projects the image of the temple outward, an image he approaches with awe and reverence. From a depth psychological perspective, Henry Corbin contends that such a form or image is needed for the psyche to grasp the concept of *Imago Templi*, the sacred Temple within. Corbin asserts, "I would say that the virtue of the *Imago Templi* lies in making us be *within ourselves outside ourselves*. For we must not confuse introspection, introversion, with contemplation: there is no contemplation without the Temple." (*Temple and Contemplation* 388) Corbin's comments summarize the archetypal significance of the Temple, which Jung experienced firsthand. Ultimately, seekers of all traditions find themselves bumping up against the powerful temple archetype at some point, which involves a dismantling of the ego self.

This theory involves a rupturing of the notion of self and other as subjective and brings one's self into pure objective form. To enter the temple is to melt object and subject together: From outside the temple, Jung recalls, "I existed in an objective form; I was what I had been and lived." (*Memories, Dreams, Reflections* 291) Jung experienced the withdrawal of his ego during the painful process of "defoliation" and what remained was Jung's Self. "I had everything that I was, and that was everything." (*Memories, Dreams, Reflections* 291) Jung experienced his pure essence, devoid of ego.

Jung's vision occurs in the imaginal realm of Corbin's *mundus imaginalis* (*'alam al-mithal*), comparable to the realm of the in-between, of the *barzakh*, as discussed elsewhere, and the Tibetan Buddhist concept of *bardo*, another example of an intermediate state. Said another way, this realm is metaphorically "between the two seas," symbolized by an isthmus such as Rama's bridge, a submerged bridge that once appears to have connected Pamban Island (India) and Sri Lanka's Mannar Island. The heart provides such an isthmus between the divine realm and everyday waking reality.

Jung did not see the temple with his physical eyes; rather, his vision was apprehended through the "eyes of his heart" in the imaginal realm. Carl Jung stepped into the *bardo,* or *barzakh,* during his heart attack and saw with the organ of perception, the heart, even as he lay unconscious. I agree with Hillman when he asserts, "This imaginal intelligence resides in the heart: 'intelligence of the heart' connotes a simultaneous knowing [. . .] by means of imagining." (*Thought of the Heart* 7) This form of knowing imaginally is not subject to the same laws of reason; rather, it is subject to the laws of Sophia, the Wisdom of the heart.

Jung's vision of the temple reveals further significant psychological elements. What began in the vision as a large stone block morphs into a sacred temple. Jung excitedly anticipates entering the temple, perceiving that he is expected and that all his questions regarding the mysteries of life are about to be disclosed to him. Outside, the yogi silently meditates while waiting for Jung's arrival. From Jung's eager anticipation, one surmises that great Wisdom is to be found inside the temple—that which has been previously unknown.

From the Sufi perspective, Corbin writes, "the *Imago Templi* is associated particularly with the representation of Wisdom, Sophia as a hypostasis [. . .] common in wisdom literature." (*Temple and Contemplation* 293) The Greek term hypostasis ὑπόστασις is the underlying essence that supports all reality as we experience it.

For the Sufis, Greeks, and other Wisdom traditions, Sophia is the underlying feminine essence that supports the physical world.

In Jung's precardiac work "The Symbolism of the Mandala," he includes a 17th-century plate, "The Mountain and the Adepts," which displays "the temple of the wise" held within a mountain and buried deep within the psyche. (*CW* 12:293) The "missing fourth" aspect, the eternal feminine wisdom, Sophia, reemerges inside the temple, however Jung remains outside. Jung later writes in *Mysterium Coniunctionis*, "it is the human soul imprisoned in the body as the *anima mundi* is in matter, and this soul undergoes the same trans-formations by death and purification, and finally by glorification, as the lapis." (*CW* 14:321) The image of the temple is a prefiguration of Jung's own individuation.

In his cardiac arrest vision image, Jung describes the door to the temple having a "wreath of bright flames" and recalls having seen such a sight at the Temple of the Holy Tooth in Ceylon.[95] In the well-known image of the dancing Nataraja Shiva, a ring of flames encircles Shiva, the destroyer in the Hindu trinity, symbolizing the element of fire that one must pass *through* for purification prior to transformation. Devastating life events that shake us to the core of our being serve as the dancing flames of Shiva that one must pass through in order to evolve to higher levels of consciousness. Through this cleansing process, old psychic patterns of thought must be extinguished before new realities can spring forward, that is, if one can withstand the flames without being destroyed.

---

95   The Temple of the Sacred Tooth Relic (Sri Dalada Maligawa) is a Buddhist temple in the city of Kandy, Sri Lanka, now Ceylon. This temple houses the Sacred Tooth relic of the Buddha.

The Role of Emotions, Psychological States, and the Coherent Heart

Heart coherence occurs when one is living in harmony with one's "cor" values, which are generated from one's heart center and aligned with the grander scheme of *anima mundi*, the soul of the world.

The relationship of stress and emotional states to heart coherence has been widely researched and documented. Paul Rosch, president of the American Institute of Stress, states, "HRV is a superb indicator of your ability to cope with both internal and external changes. It is, in fact, the most accurate predictor of sudden death and the most accurate reflector of stress."[96] For the purposes of this book, I focus on emotional states that are generally within one's own control, as opposed to conditions and disorders of brain chemistry such as clinical depression or severe anxiety.

There is a direct relationship between negative and positive emotions, states of consciousness and HRV. Changes in ANS are strongly influenced by emotions: Negative emotions decrease HRV by suppressing parasympathetic branch activity, while positive emotions increase HRV by engaging the parasympathetic branch. Thus, HRV monitoring can be used to determine not just ANS health and pliability but also one's psychological state.

Although it has been shown in many studies that emotional well-being and stress reduction can provide defenses against many disease states, the patient's psyche is not typically factored into the healing equation in Western medicine. Many specialists may treat a single patient, and yet the contributing role of stress is not probed sufficiently. Since intense or prolonged stress is a precursor for most disease states, an important avenue for intervention is missed. Instead, the patient's state of mind and psyche are either ignored or medicated.

Moreover, even if healing occurs, the process has sidestepped an opportunity for psychic transformation. The body may be "repaired," but the psyche is not.

---

96   https://www.earthinginstitute.net/nurturing-the-nervous-system-heart-connection/

The emotional resiliency of a person is directly related to how well he or she manages his or her own response to stimuli experienced through sense perceptions. Humans are subject to both pleasant and unpleasant incoming stimuli, most of which are outside of one's control. It is our *reaction* to the incoming triggers that determines whether we will experience stress and disease, or calm and repose. For example, how do you react to being cut off in traffic? Someone who has learned to manage their reactions simply notices, brakes or changes lanes, and carries on. Someone who is easily triggered may, in contrast, experience "road rage" or fume for hours afterward.

Jung talked a lot about complexes. A complex is feeling-toned autonomous psychic content that forms during traumatic events and which is too painful to keep in one's conscious awareness. When someone's "buttons get pushed," it is often followed by a statement such as "I don't know what got into me." A complex is the button that gets pushed. It can be thought of as a psychic blister; it protects a sore spot that you don't want to get bumped. If you have ever recognized that you've gotten caught up in an activated complex, the "seed" begins to bloom into patterns of behavior that are unique to the complex itself. Once activated or bumped, the complex takes over and generally has to run its course. In a sense, the individual may temporarily lose control of him or herself. Through latter reflection or analysis, this process or chain reaction can be realized and perhaps prevented in the future. When you are able to distance yourself from your complexes, you begin to put distance between the resulting chain reaction of emotion and events and bring conscious awareness into the process.[97] Once you consciously recognize the cause-effect dynamics, it begins to release the intensity of the complex.

The unseen challenge is that most people are living in a chronic stress response of high sympathetic activity—which in Eastern healing modalities would be called the masculine, or *yang*—and have squelched their parasympathetic activity (which we can think of as *yin*, feminine). This phenomenon shows up as high-functioning anxiety and

---

97 This is one reason why meditation and mindfulness practices are so effective; the practitioner learns to recognize the "gap" between the thought and an ensuing emotional response.

stress-induced depression, or in *Kundalini* yogic terms, "cold depression." Figure 21 in Chapter Three demonstrates what these conditions look like on HRV feedback graphs. When sympathetic activity is high, the "masculine" branch of the ANS is overwhelming the "feminine" branch. This is often experienced as feelings of overwhelm, anxiety, and cold depression.

A feeling of calm registers higher on the coherence spectrum than either anxiety or depression. The highest states of heart coherence have, in my experience, come from generating a neutral mindset void of emotional triggers: the still point, or *Shuniya* in yogic terms. Such a mindset creates the signature "sine wave" pattern in the heart rhythm pattern. Breath work can also induce higher states of heart rhythm coherence when respiratory stimulation of the vagus nerve activates the parasympathetic branch of the ANS. Simply slowing and deepening the breath or breathing deeply through the left nostril only are effective starting points for optimizing heart rhythm coherence.

We can train ourselves to achieve this state. After years of HRV feedback practice, I have found that simply sitting on my meditation mat and setting a mental intention to move into a state of high coherence causes my mind-body to go immediately into a coherent state, as shown in Figure 27. This is almost a daily occurrence. With consistent practice, the body anticipates what it is supposed to do, and the desired state is rapidly achieved.

Improving heart rhythm coherence allows people to regain a sense of control and responsibility over their health and healing outcomes. I call such somatic coherence the "*somatic coniunctionis.*"[98] First, the sympathetic and parasympathetic branches of the ANS marry or cohere. In such a state, we are better able to integrate our inner divisions of masculine and feminine for the psychological *coniunctionis*. This inner union in turn allows the mind-body to operate in unison with the larger magnetic fields of the Earth and sun—to pulsate with the *anima mundi*, the soul of the world.

---

98   As heart coherence increases the other weaker oscillating fields of the body, including brain functions, sync of with the with the heart's stronger electromagnetic field. As the systems of the body work together instead of energetically fighting one another they perform more efficiently, individually and collectively as "one body."

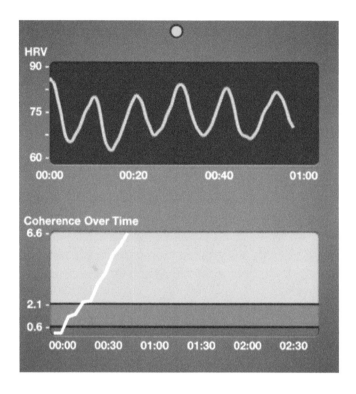

Figure 27 Setting Intention Leads to Rapid Rise in Heart Coherence. Image credit: Author using HeartMath® iPhone Inner Balance app.

In the highest state of coherence, I theorize that the person experiences the *Mysterium coniunctionis,* the feeling of being one with all. Thus, somatic coherence creates the right conditions for the psychological marriage of archetypal forces and ultimately, for wholeness at every level.

Techniques for achieving heart coherence are based in scientific methodology (HRV), depth psychological techniques, and spiritual disciplines such as mindfulness and meditation/prayer practices. Instead of the cause-and-effect paradigm of Western science (do x treatment and get result y), we start with the end in mind: heart coherence. There are many paths to optimizing heart coherence covered in the rest of this book. Whatever brings you into a state of high heart coherence, or optimal HRV, is the right therapy for you.

Ocean Breath Meditation, *Ujjayi Pranayam*

"Ocean Breath" or *Ujjayi Pranayama* is a pranayam that is used in several yogic traditions. Also known as Conquerors Breath and Sounder's Breath.

Tune-in (Vocalization)[99]

Chant three times: *Ong Namo Guru Dev Namo*

Posture
Sit either on the floor in easy pose (cross-legged) or in a chair. Ensure that your spine is straight. Tuck you chin in slightly into "neck-lock" (*jalandhar bandh*).

Hand Position (Mudra)
Relaxed hands.

Vocalization (Mantra)
Silent, listen to the sound of the breath only.

Eye Position (Dhrist)
Eyes are closed and focused at the third eye point (between the eyebrows).

Breath Pattern
Begin breathing as if you were attempting to fog a mirror or eyeglasses with the breath from your mouth, then move the breathing pattern to your nose and close your mouth. Listen for

---

99   Tuning In: Translation: I bow to the infinite teacher within, and open myself to the infinite source of wisdom, healing, and creativity within me. Before beginning any *Kundalini* yoga practice, "tune-in" with the Adi Mantra, which sets an intention to connect with your infinite Self within. This also helps to set practice time apart from your normal daily routine. Tuning-in is a call to your higher Self, the healer within, and aligns you with Infinite source. Set an intention for healing your stress and anxiety as you connect with your inner Heart's Wisdom.

the "sound of the ocean" in the nasal cavity and back of neck to confirm that you are doing it correctly.

Visualization

Still the mind and focus on the breath, minimizing emotional interference. This subtle action stimulates the portion of the ventral vagus nerve which runs through the neck.

Time

Continue for 11 minutes or up to 31 minutes (it takes 11 minutes to begin to affect the ANS).

Contraindication

If you begin to feel dizzy, stop the exercise.

Optional HRV Biofeedback

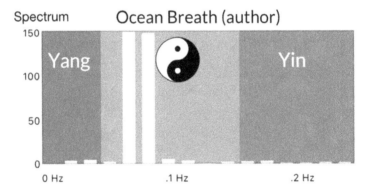

Figure 28 HRV Biofeedback during Ocean Breath. Image credit: Author using HeartMath® Inner Balance iPhone app.

CHAPTER FIVE

Descent to the Underworld

*"I think, literally, because you have cracked the chest,
you are vulnerable, totally, for the first time since birth."*

— Robin Williams[100]

The late actor Robin Williams articulated what is a common experience after heart surgery or a major cardiac event. A state of vulnerability reigns, contributing to the traumatic nature of the situation and increasing the subsequent risk of depression as well as additional cardiac events.

The body is wounded when the rib cage is cracked open to gain access to the heart, when the groin is cut into to harvest vessels for a coronary bypass, or through death of a portion of the heart muscle during a heart attack. But it is not just the physical body that is wounded during major cardiac events; the psyche is also traumatized. This wounding can have devastating effects.

Depression: The Dark Side of Low Heart Coherence

Heart disease often evokes depression; depression has been shown to increase the occurrence of heart disease. Although the connection remains somewhat unclear, heart attack survivors and depression frequently go hand in hand. As one authority puts it, "Recovering from a heart attack is tough enough without facing depression.

---

100   "Opening Wide His [Repaired] Heart"

Yet that's exactly what happens to nearly half of heart attack survivors,"[101] including patients who were not prone to depression prior to their heart attack.

One study suggested that "reductions in HRV observed among depressed older adults are driven by the effects of antidepressant medications. [. . .] Depression is a known risk factor for the development of cardiovascular disease (CVD) and an independent predictor of poor prognosis following a cardiac event (Lett *et al.* 2004). Alterations in the autonomic nervous system (ANS) including a reduction in heart rate variability (HRV) may partly explain the increased risk of CVD, since low HRV is a known risk factor for myocardial infarction,[102] arrhythmias, and cardiac mortality (Tsuji *et al.* 1994; Dekker *et al.* 2000; Carney & Freedland, 2009)."

Researchers have found that "Major depression in patients hospitalized following an MI is an independent risk factor for mortality at 6 months. Its impact is at least equivalent to that of . . . history of previous MI."[103] In other words, to be severely depressed after a heart attack is equivalent to having had *two* heart attacks in terms of the impact on survival. Researchers also recognized that ". . . depressed patients with cardiac disease have reduced heart rate variability, suggesting that depression may be associated with changes in sympathetic-parasympathetic balance" and concluded ". . . if sympathetic drive is increased or vagal tone is decreased, depression could be strongly proarrhythmogenic [producing or promoting arrhythmia] in patients at risk for ventricular arrhythmias."[104] The ANS, ventricular arrhythmias, and vagal tone all play a role in post-heart-attack depression.

---

101   https://www.health.harvard.edu/press_releases/depression-and-heart-disease
102   Refer to the 2018 Fourth Universal Definition of Myocardial Infarction from the European Society of Cardiology (ESC)/ American College of Cardiology (ACC)/ American Heart Association (AHA)/ World Heart Federation (WHF) Task Force for the Universal Definition of Myocardial Infarction
103   "Depression and 18-Month Prognosis After Myocardial Infarction," Nancy Frasure-Smith, PhD et al., (JAMA 1993 Oct 20;270(15):1819-25)
104   (Circulation. 1995; 91: 999-1005 doi: 10.1161/01.CIR.91.4.999).

Many other studies have confirmed the relationship between low HRV and poor cardiovascular outcomes.[105] One researcher at the Heart and Vascular Medicine department at the Johns Hopkins Institute, Roy Ziegelstein, noted, "A percentage of people with no history of depression become depressed after a heart attack or after developing heart failure. And people with depression but no previously detected heart disease, seem to develop heart disease at a higher rate than the general population." Although Ziegelstein acknowledges that it is difficult to prove that heart disease leads to depression, "what we can say with certainty is that depression and heart disease often occur together."[106]

Compounding the problem, antidepressant medicines may lower HRV. Researchers investigating the relationship between antidepressants and reduced HRV reported that ". . . reductions in HRV observed among depressed older adults are driven by the effects of antidepressant medications."[107] Depression, antidepressants, and HRV form a complex matrix that must be considered before pharmaceutical intervention. Heart patients contemplating antidepressants following a major cardiac event can ask their provider about monitoring HRV using a diagnostic 24-hour Holter device to assess the appropriateness of taking such medications. Such data can help the physician and the patient to make informed choices.

While Western medicine views post-heart-attack depression as a treatable medical disorder, depth psychologists approach depression as a call by the psyche for change, growth, and transformation. The cardiac event survivor cannot *will* his or her health back, which may be experienced as a defeat for the ego as one loses control over one's own fate. Hillman reminds us that "the true revolution begins in the individual who can be true to his or her depression."[i] In other words, depression is a wake-up call, asking the individual to acknowledge his or her deepest longings and what is getting in the way.

---

105   "Depressive Symptoms and Heart Rate Variability in Postmenopausal Women," Chin K. Kim, MD, et. al.

106   (Ziegelstein, 2019). Post Heart Attack Depression: The Soul's Cry

107   (Antidepressants strongly influence the relationship between depression and heart rate variability: findings from The Irish Longitudinal Study on Ageing (TILDA), 2015).

Symbolic messages can emerge from psyche during and after a traumatic cardiac event, as demonstrated by Roland's case study provided at the end of this book. The wounding of the physical heart evokes a kind of consciousness not available at other times. This new awareness can appear in dreams, synchronicities, or visions. Even if one does not understand the symbolic significance of these images as they arise, journaling or drawing them as best as one can at the time is useful. Allow your heart, the organ of perception, to guide the process and refrain from the temptation to take the images literally. Working with a trained depth psychologist or Jungian analyst can help you tease the meaning out of the *prima materia*, the raw images.

Jung's own depression after a severe heart attack (in 1944) and subsequent work with his visions provides a rich example of how one can work with the images that arise following the wounding of the heart. In Jung's case, this work led him to coherence of the masculine and feminine polarities within.

Jung's Heart Attack Visions:
Image and Individuation

Like many heart attack survivors, Jung suffered a depression so severe that it took him three weeks to decide if he really wanted to continue to live.[108] But he had the wisdom to recognize that depression can provide a unique portal into the *imaginal heart*, the source of archetypal images, providing a pathway for individuation. Jung was also a student of the ancient art of alchemy (the precursor of much of our modern science) and recognized the opportunity for turning the "lead" of his depression into "gold"—the chance for him to reengage with a life of meaning, turning the acorn of his being into the powerful oak tree.

Archetypal messages are perhaps best understood and mined while undergoing a depression, before seeking to eradicate it. In Jung's case, he spent three weeks working with visions before he

---

108   Memories, Dreams, Reflections

recovered his will to live. During the days, Jung suffered from an intense depression, but each night he had visions that he described in terms of bliss, light, beauty, and intensity of emotion.

Engaging with and fully experiencing his visions created a liminal space between his old life and the new one of his true destiny, with a profound impact on the course of his work *and* life. As he said:

> It was only after the illness that I understood how important it is to affirm one's destiny. In this way we forge an ego that does not break down when incomprehensible things happen; an ego that endures, that endures the truth, and that is capable of coping with the world and with fate.[109]

The archetypal images that arose in Jung's consciousness during and after his heart attack provided fertile ground for his creative genius. By 1944, Jung had produced many impressive volumes of work, but his most significant publications—including *Aion* (1951), "Answer to Job" (1952), "Synchronicity: An Acausal Connecting Principle" (1952), and his crowning achievement, the *Mysterium Coniunctionis* (1952), were completed after his heart attack.

Jung's visions consisted of "encounters" and visions he experienced upon losing consciousness during his heart attack and during the subsequent convalescent period. His images ranged from viewing the Earth from several miles high, where Jung described the continents below[110] to an encounter with his doctor in his "primal form."[111] The ecstatic nighttime visions provided a sharp contrast to his daytime depression, in which the world appeared gray and "boxlike." He found everyday reality to be one of separateness, opposed to his experience of the coherent state of Universal oneness through the internal sacred marriage of the masculine and feminine principles.

---

109   Ibid, p. 297.
110   It would be 25 more years before the first images of the earth from space were available to humankind.
111   Interested readers are encouraged to read Jung's autobiographical *Memories, Dreams, Reflections* to take in the full richness of his experience.

Many of his nighttime visions were preceded by what he referred to as a "ritual meal" of kosher dishes prepared by his nurse, who took on the essence of an older Jewish woman around whom shone a blue halo. The color blue has a significant place in alchemical and spiritual symbolism. Blue is the color of the ineffable, the limitless sky (from our perspective on Earth), the robes of Mary, or an elusive or rare flower.

Hillman described blue as representing the soul's transition out of the black (*nigredo*) phase of ego death—what many call the dark night of the soul—to the white phase (*albedo*) of redemption, the synthesis of masculine and feminine. Blue stands for the imaginal realm as if betwixt and between *nigredo* and *albedo*. The woman who shines with a blue light recalls the "bride, Mary (as intercessor), moon, dawn, and dove."[112] She is a precursor of what is to come for Jung, his personal *coniunctionis,* the completed individuation process.

One key vision for Jung was that of the wedding of Malchuth and Tifereth in the garden of pomegranates, the *Pardes Rimmonim*. In the Kabbalistic tradition, Malchuth (also known as Shekinah, the feminine) and Tifereth (masculine) are two of the 10 manifestations of the Godhead. In his description of this vision, Jung spoke of himself as *being* the marriage of Malchuth and Tifereth. His interior divine feminine and masculine were joined in the *hierosgamos*, or holy union.

Jung identified Malchuth as "the underlying feminine principle," portraying her as abandoned and a widow when Tifereth is not with her, but a "watered garden" when she and Tifereth are together.[113] He commented, "In this wicked world ruled by evil Tifereth is *not* united with Malchuth. But the coming Messiah will reunite the King with the Queen and this mating will restore to God his original unity."[114] The pairing of the feminine and masculine restores unity. This myth represents what was unfolding within Jung's psyche following his cardiac event—a recognition of his internal estrangement or dissociation from his own internal feminine principle, his *anima*. In order

---

112   Hillman, *Alchemical Psychology, 154*
113   *Mysterium Coniunctionis.* (1989, p. 22).
114   Ibid, (1989, p. 23)

for him to successfully complete his personal individuation process, the separation was required for healing.

Thus, Jung's visions allowed him to reengage with his creative imagination and his *daimon*, his creative genius, at a profound level. His process offers a guide to others for engaging with their own dream material, allowing one's own personal mythology to emerge from psyche. A heart attack brings one close to death, and the juxtaposition between the beauty of life and the terror of death enhances both. In the myth of Psyche and Eros, Psyche's beauty is considered more powerful than Aphrodite's because of her mortalness—her proximity to death. It is Psyche's mortality that intensifies her fleeting beauty in a manner not available to Aphrodite, an immortal goddess. A major cardiac event can feel like a brush with death, causing great fear; yet for many, the recognition of one's own mortality makes life all the more precious. This was the case for Jung—and Roland, as seen in his case study.

From the moment of birth, death is one's continual companion. Recognizing this, one has the choice either to embrace a life of meaning or to live life mechanically, going through the motions. The awareness of death creates a sense of urgency to follow one's own destiny, to avoid what T. S. Eliot called the "wasteland," a life lived from ego rather than from one's heart center, one's authentic Self.

Jung said, "There is an extraordinary distance from the head to the heart, a distance of ten, twenty, thirty years, or a whole lifetime."[115] The metaphoric journey is one of remembering and unveiling the feminine, that which seeks to allow rather than force, to listen rather than speak, and to restore coherence in a world out of balance. It begins by listening to the voice inside of you that urges you to go in a specific direction. The path is challenging. However, going with the flow of what other people want you to do, or pursuing work just for the money, may solidify into a life that becomes very difficult to change. The prison walls of a mortgage, student loan debt, or family obligations are not easily altered. The physical body is affected by our choices and will pay the price of a life lived out of alignment with *cor* values.

---

115   Jung, C. G., *The Psychology of Kundalini Yoga*

As Jung succinctly put it, "Anyone who takes the sure road is as good as dead."[116] Individuation requires doing the difficult work of confronting the unconscious psyche. A major cardiac event, like other traumas, provides a temporary opening that may not be available during ordinary times.

EXPERIENTIAL PRACTICE

The Rainmaker Story, Expanding the Rings of Coherence

In addition to dreams and visions, Jung's journey was influenced by synchronicities, his term for "meaningful coincidences" that demonstrate an unseen connection between an internal state and the world around us. For example, perhaps you start thinking about someone you haven't thought of for years, the phone rings, and you hear their voice on the other end of the line. One synchronicity involved Richard Wilhelm[117], a contemporary of Jung's who had a significant personal and professional impact on Jung's life. In this particular case, Wilhelm passed along the story of the Rainmaker at a critical juncture in Jung's life.

At the heart of psyche-soma healing lay the concept of synchronicity, the *tao*, and coherence. In Jung's synchronicity theory, he observed that "psychological laws rule external events [. . .]" The oft retelling of Professor Wilhelm's rainmaker story encapsulates Jung's synchronicity theory and presents a model for postmodern humanity. Denying that he caused the precipitation, the rainmaker said that when he was called to the village he was "not in right order" (coherence) as he had been when he left home. By bringing himself back into "right order," the external event of the drought also fell back into "right order," a synchronistic event. "The Rainmaker" story illustrates

---

116 *Memories, Dreams, Reflections*, 297.
117 (10 May 1873 – 2 March 1930) was a German sinologist, theologian, missionary, and translator of the *I Ching*.

the paradoxical relationship between right order within oneself and "right order" in the community, and nature. Jung contended, "Tao is the condition which is in tune with the ordinances of heaven, a complete expression of the order that rules heaven and earth." The rainmaker did not *cause* the snow to fall; rather, he harmonized internal events into a state of coherence, thus allowing spontaneous acausal events to occur. The interconnectedness between humans and their environment is linked—for better or worse.

The interrelationship between the *tao*, coherence, and synchronicity results from internal harmonization, which ultimately leads to a synchronicity of *anima mundi* and the collective heart—the throb of creation itself.

The "Rainmaker of Kiau-Tchou" story goes as follows:

> There was a great drought where Wilhelm lived; for months there had not been a drop of rain and the situation became catastrophic. The Catholics made processions, the Protestants made prayers, and the Chinese burned joss sticks and shot off guns to frighten away the demons of the drought, but with no result.

> Finally, the Chinese said: We will fetch the rainmaker. And from another province, a dried up old man appeared. The only thing he asked for was a quiet little house somewhere, and there he locked himself in for three days. On the fourth day clouds gathered and there was a great snowstorm at the time of the year when no snow was expected, an unusual amount, and the town was so full of rumors about the wonderful rain maker that Wilhelm went to ask the man how he did it. In true European fashion he said: "They call you the rain maker, will you tell me how you made the snow?" And the little Chinaman said: "I did not make the snow, I am not responsible." "But what have you done these three days?" "Oh, I can explain that. I come from another country where things are in order.

Here they are out of order, they are not as they should be by the ordnance of heaven. Therefore, the whole country is not in *Tao*, and I am also not in the natural order of things because I am in a disordered country. So I had to wait three days until I was back in *Tao*, and then naturally the rain came.[118]"

Note that the Rainmaker claimed that he didn't do anything. He simply allowed himself to realign with the natural order of the *tao*. Similarly, when one learns how to become coherent both physically and psychologically, life begins to appear in "right order." The missing feminine reappears between the third and fourth day, unpredictably, as snow. The feminine unveils herself in ways that we may not expect— but is just what is needed.

1. In what ways do you see you own state of inner heart rhythm coherence affecting the people around you?

2. In what ways do you see your coherence levels of your family affecting your community or vice versa?

3. How do "rings of coherence" affect the greater order of *anima mundi*, the soul of the world?

Before I close this chapter I would like to share my story regarding a sequence of related experiences that caused my heart to close for several years. The purpose of my sharing is to inspire others to believe that there is another way to live after devastating events occur, and our past is a story that we can perpetuate or transcend. The choice is ours to make.

Anne's Story

My own descent into the underworld, which initiated the closing of my heart for many years, could have kept me in victimhood for the rest of my life, while repeating variations on a theme thinking it was the fault of others. I have come to believe that we attract what we are

---

118   Jung, *Visions Seminars* 333

vibrating out, specifically in relation to low heart rhythm coherence as discussed in Section I. There is no good guy or bad guy in this story, only two people living life from their pain bodies. The misapprehension of low self-esteem gets ingrained in many children, as it did for me. Ancestral lines tend to unconsciously perpetuate traumas. Until the root causes are brought into conscious awareness and healed, the cycle of self-destructive choices will likely continue. As I wrote this reflection 40 year later, I feel only compassion for the young woman and the young man whose only fault was being unaware and unconscious.

The gold of transformation lies in the lead of our traumatic life experiences. The painful alchemical process of engaging with our unconscious material is necessary, but only to a point. In the end, the most effective healing strategy that I experienced required me to get my body into the healing process, as talk therapy yielded limited and unsustained results. *Kundalini* yoga, which includes meditation and *pranayama*, were the portals of transformation that allowed me to discharge the deeply lodged psychological wounds, heal my nervous system, and literally rewire my brain. An unexpected "byproduct" of this work was spiritual awakening. *Kundalini* yoga is only one path of many; people need to work with healing modalities that they resonate with the best.

To begin my story, it was late February, and I was faced with the most difficult task of my life, at least up to that point. I received a call from my then father-in-law telling me that my sister-in-law had been shot by an unknown assailant and that I needed to call my husband and let him know what happened. That was the hardest call I ever made; his sister was just 21, newly married, and living oversees with her military husband, and now she was gone. Understandably, yet sadly, my husband closed down and withdrew from me emotionally in the days and weeks following the tragedy. Everyone handles sudden shocks differently, but the pain of being shut out from someone you love going through an incredibly difficult loss is another profound loss in itself.

Due to the nature of the incident, her body was detained in Europe, leaving the family to cope with this violent tragedy with many unanswered questions. Every day the family would gather and console one another as best as we knew how. One evening, only four days after her death, I left the family vigil to go home ahead of my husband. He had been my first boyfriend, my first lover, the only man I ever knew.

Now at home up in our bedroom, I heard footsteps coming up the stairs, happy that my husband was home. He had still been withdrawn, and I needed him. Stepping out into the hallway to greet him, I was met by a red ski mask and a foot-long knife.

Cornered into the bedroom, I had no chance of escape. My mind flashed that this was the man who killed my sister-in-law. Without thinking, I instinctively lunged at my attacker screaming, "You're not going to kill me too," and tried to get the knife away from him. Instead, my finger slipped around the blade as he struck me to the ground. The knife dropped, and I surrendered my efforts. Fortunately, he had no intention of raping me; this man's modus operando was to terrorize women and "perform" in front of them. With the recent rape and murder of my sister-in-law, my mind had mind conflated time and space during the encounter.

When my husband arrived home, detectives and squad cars were around the house; they had been trying to catch this guy for a while, a known stalker of women. While I was being attacked, my husband was down the street with another woman, getting comfort perhaps the only way he knew how. It wasn't the attack per se that started to close my heart but the lack of closeness and support, especially when I pleaded with husband to get off the night shift at the hospital, at least until I could recover emotionally. But he refused. I was terrified to be alone in the house, and as the darkness grew every evening, I knew that my attacker was still out there.

Time passed, I had surgery on my hand, and gradually life seemed to find a new normal. My husband and I seemed to be finding our way again, and within the year I became pregnant. We were both happy about it, and there was so much to look forward to, that is until the second blow hit me. At seven months into the pregnancy, I went into early labor and was hospitalized. The baby and I were stabilizing, but the doctor informed me that I would have to have bedrest for the duration of the pregnancy.

While still in the hospital, my husband announced that he didn't want to be married anymore and so when I was discharged from the hospital I went back home to my parents. Shutting down when life got challenging was his coping mechanism, but I had to bear the consequences, or so it seemed at the time.

The nature of trauma is interesting because it seems to me that we have a psychological "buffer," but once a certain threshold is reached, there is a breaking point of sorts. For me, the final straw was finding the *Evita!* playbill, a Broadway play that I had been waiting to see, in the glove box of my blue Camaro. This final event flipped some switch inside me and closed what was left of my heart. I finished the one year of college I had left and left the marriage. And from the depths of my being, I told myself that I would never be dependent on a man again. And thus began my professional life where I stayed in my head, made good money, and life was within my control, or so it seemed. I have dedicated the past many years to healing my heart and rebuilding my self-esteem and transforming my life.

Until we recognize and take responsibility for the damage caused by traumatic events that we have endured, we will tend to repeat the patterns of choices and behaviors. Similar core issues, a new cast of characters and patterns repeat. We can either stay with our stories and blame others and our circumstances, or we can find the courage to heal.

The gold of transformation lies hidden within our traumas, and although I would never to choose to repeat these "life lessons," I would not have the depth, strength, and awareness that I do today. Like the Rainmaker, I have brought myself back into "right order." It is worth the effort and pain of going directly into the mouth of the dragon and conquering the fears and consciously rebirthing the authentic you.

The Archetypal Heart

For a New Beginning

In out-of-the-way places of the heart,
Where your thoughts never think to wander,
This beginning has been quietly forming,
Waiting until you were ready to emerge.

For a long time it has watched your desire,
Feeling the emptiness growing inside you,
Noticing how you willed yourself on,
Still unable to leave what you had outgrown.

It watched you play with the seduction of safety
And the gray promises that sameness whispered,
Heard the waves of turmoil rise and relent,
Wondered would you always live like this.

Then the delight, when your courage kindled,
And out you stepped onto new ground,
Your eyes young again with energy and dream,
A path of plenitude opening before you.

Though your destination is not yet clear
You can trust the promise of this opening;
Unfurl yourself into the grace of beginning
That is at one with your life's desire.

Awaken your spirit to adventure;
Hold nothing back, learn to find ease in risk;
Soon you will be home in a new rhythm,
For your soul senses the world that awaits you.

— John O' Donohue

CHAPTER SIX

Archetypes and Patterns

"The archetypal images decide the fate of man."

– Jung[119]

In Chapter Three, we explored how heart coherence can be expressed in numbers and displayed as a serpentine sine waveform. Now, we move to an archetypal discussion of how the heart expresses itself through symbolism. As the great Sufi poets have taught, the heart is an organ of perception that accesses wisdom beyond the confines of the rational mind. This happens when one enters into the imaginal realm, a place that is not a place but rather a state betwixt and between. In this chapter and the next, we explore the archetypal symbolism of numbers, sine waves, spirals, and helixes. These patterns reverberate throughout nature and psyche—for psyche *is* nature.

What Is an Archetype?

The term archetype evolved from Plato's notion of *eidos* (Greek for form, or essence). Plato viewed the ideal or model Form as existing in a transcendent state—that is to say, sitting "above" the seen world. This concept was defined by Plato in *Timaeus* (360 B.C.E.). In brief, he stated that there exists one perfect form or idea, of which everything in the phenomenal realm is an imperfect copy. Think of a tree for example. Thousands of species of trees exist and of all the different physical manifestations of trees, no one single tree is perfect. What unites the many variations of trees, i.e. shapes, size, color, and fragrance, is its

---

119   Jung, *CW* 18, vol. 18, "The Travaitock Lectures," page 163

underlying essence, or Form. The trees' "suchness" is an abstraction that exists only in the nonvisible world, a world that cannot be touched, tasted, or seen. Plato's theory of Forms is metaphysical, above the physical and visible world. Ask most any child to draw a tree, and he or she will come up with some expression of the Form, its embodied knowledge of the Form itself. This is also the playing field of the American Transcendentalists such as Ralph Waldo Emerson who wrote about *reality* beyond the seen world.

The ancient Chinese also believed that transcendent Forms sit above the physical world and expressed the unseen reality using 64 hexagrams, which were made up of combinations of eight stacked lines consisting of unbroken (masculine) and broken (feminine) lines. Hexagrams are combinations of masculine and feminine polarities that point to a reality beyond the seen world and the cosmos beyond. For example, six unbroken lines represents maximum *yang*, Father/Heaven, and its counterpart, six broken lines representing *yin*, Mother/Earth. Even the hexagrams themselves only point to the underlying Form of Father or Mother, and the sons and daughters in between. The Forms are constant and unchanging, like underlying Ultimate reality.

As the term is used by depth psychologists, an archetype may be thought of as a distinct pattern or structural potentiality held within the unconscious and expressed into the conscious psyche as images, ideas, and symbols. But each reflected image appears as a slightly imperfect "copy" of the original Form.

One of Jung's foundational theories was that humankind partakes in a collective pool of archetypes dating back to prehistoric times. This level of psyche antecedes the individual psyche and contains an amalgam of forms from humanity's ancestors. This shared collective layer, which Jung called the collective unconscious, was built from the earliest emergence of human consciousness; Jung referred to it as the "two million year old [hu]man within" each of us.

As he put it:

> In addition to our immediate consciousness . . . there exists a second psychic system of a collective universal and impersonal nature, which is identical in all individuals.

This collective unconscious does not develop individually but is inherited. It consists of pre-existent forms, the archetypes...[120]

Thus, the collective unconscious is the common field of autonomous archetypes shared by all humans.

One may think of a human mother, for example. The perfect form or archetype of Mother does not change; however, images of her are expressed both culturally (e.g., Isis, Virgin Mary, Brigid) and personally as one's biological or adoptive mother. In "Psychological Aspects of the Mother Archetype," Jung clarified that "the archetype in itself is empty and purely formal, nothing but *facultas praeformandi*, a possibility of representation which is given *a priori*."[121]

Archetypes are *potential* and cannot be directly witnessed. While the archetypes underlying the images are universal and shared collectively among humankind, the images released into consciousness during a dream or flash of insight are specific to the individual or culture within a historical window of time. Thus, images of human mothers take on the cultural norms of their times in regard to appearance, work, and ways of being in the world reflecting their generation. But the archetype of Mother itself is without form.

Jung pointed out, "The primordial image, elsewhere also termed archetype, is always collective, i.e., it is at least common to entire peoples or epochs."[122] Mythologies and folk tales elucidate universally held motifs (mythogems) in unique cultural dress. Creation myths frequently contain two complementary and opposing elements, which emerge from a unitive state into one of multiplicity. Dreams and nonordinary states of consciousness—including, as shown in the example of Jung's heart attack visions, disease states—are also rich sources of such images.

---

120   *CW* 9i "The Concept of the Collective Unconscious," par 90
121   *CW* 9i, ¶ 155
122   *CW* 6, ¶ 747

Archetypes may therefore be thought of as psychic seeds: image and pattern generators that are inherited and collectively shared among humankind. Another way to think of archetypes is as blueprints showing the dimensionalities and design of a building. How different people build the idea into reality can be unique. Another metaphor, one that Jung used, is the lattice of crystalline structures. "Equally, I believe, the word 'archetype' is thoroughly characteristic of the structural forms that underlie consciousness as the crystal lattice underlies the crystallization process." (C. G. Jung, Letters Volume 1, 1906-1950, page 418) The lattice itself is not a physical thing, you cannot see or measure it, yet it dictates how crystals form. Similarly, an archetype provides the underlying Form but not the psychical contents itself.

In 21st-century terminology, we can think of the collective pool of archetypes as a common "database" of forms inherent in the human psyche. We must also be on the lookout for new archetypal images arising from psyche in the midst of chaos, whether such chaos results from personal chronic stress, heart dis-ease, personal transformational experiences, or the tumultuous and stressful times we find ourselves in. From the depths of psyche, individually and collectively, new archetypal images for healing ourselves and the Earth are emerging.

What stimulates the release of archetypal images is mysterious. Pre-Enlightenment cultures often saw the gods as inspiring such images. For example, if an ancient Greek dreamt of war, the dream came from Ares, the god of war. The idea that dreams come from the divine is common across many cultures; even Descartes, the father of the Enlightenment, credited some of his most important ideas to a dream from God.

Depth psychologists believe it is the unconscious psyche attempting to communicate with the rational mind. Most people have experienced dream images, images resulting from unconscious psychic processes. A dream containing the image of an ocean, for example, carries the universal symbolism of the unconscious mind. For one person, the experience may be blissful, as when the sun sparkling on blue-green water generates peaceful feelings. For another person, the archetypal image of ocean may manifest as a menacing threat through images of increasingly large waves ready to engulf him or her.

Number: The Archetype of Order

"Number thereby throws a bridge across the gap between the physically knowable and the imaginary. In this manner it operates as a still largely unexplored midpoint between myth (the psychic) and reality (the physical), at the same time both quantitative and qualitative, representational and irrepresentational."

– Carl Jung[123]

From a Jungian perspective, number is the primal archetype of order that traverses the physical and psychical, bringing higher possibilities for transformation and healing. Jung's conjecture was that "It may well be the most primitive element of order in the human mind [. . .] thus we define number psychologically as an archetype of order which has become conscious."[124] In other words, numbers are universal symbols or archetypes that express themselves personally and collectively in a myriad of ways that most people understand to some degree. Numbers provide a window into psyche and matter, one that is infinite in nature and crosses the limitations of time and space.

You either believe you are connected to something infinite or you don't. Yet people holding to either point of view can agree that the universe is a mathematical unfolding. Then we come to the notion that a mathematical point lies outside the realm of space, for it occupies no position in the physical world. In other words, *a point lies outside of reality as we know it.*

Numbers belong to the physical world *and* beyond.

Numbers are archetypes of order as each unique number belongs to the greater continuum of the infinite number line. The full

---

123   *CW* Vol X ¶¶ 775-776
124   *On Synchronicity* par 870, p 45

implications of infinity, ∞, lie beyond the scope of human intellect or rational mind. Consider the number π (Pi), which has been calculated to a million digits (3.14159265359 . . .). It is an irrational number[125] that is infinite and yet constant (Archimedes' constant the ratio between the circumference and diameter of a circle.)

Jung wrote extensively about the numbers 1–4 as representing a psychological progression of development. The mandala (see Figure 37 for an example), which contains an inherent quaternity (represented as 12, 3, 6, 9 on the clock), was a central theme in his work regarding the union of opposites as it pertains to the individuation process. Intuitively he understood that "In the last analysis, the mystery of the *unus mundus* [one reality or in modern language, unified field], resides in the nature of number."[126] He believed that there is an underlying unity, and number is the bridge between the imaginal and the physical. The numerical expression of heart rhythm coherence[127] takes the form of a spiral sine wave, as we have seen, and serves as the *unus mundus* [Latin for one world] that underlies the duality between science and spirituality.

Many Wisdom traditions teach that there are primal masculine and feminine archetypal patterns and forces within nature; the union of these opposites is what brings matter into existence. For millennia, civilizations have used numbers as an ordering principle to assist people in understanding where they in relation to the greater universal order. From the ancient Taoist *I Ching* to the Yoruba *Ifa* divination system, people have used numerology systems to identify the relationship between themselves and an overall higher order at a specific point in time, a unique spiritual expression of the infinite.

The union of opposites is at play throughout nature. At the most basic level of matter, the atom, electrons carry a negative charge and

---

125   A number that can be expressed as an infinite decimal with no set of consecutive digits repeating itself indefinitely and that cannot be expressed as the quotient of two integers. Merriam Webster Dictionary https://www.merriam-webster.com/dictionary/irrational%20number

126   Von Franz, Marie Louise. *Number and Time* 54

127   Optimal coherence is approximately 0.1 Hz on the HeartMath® scale

protons carry a positive charge. The entire digital system of computer code is made of combinations of 1s and 0s, on and off. If the balance isn't just right, the code won't operate as intended. The cosmos, according to Taoism, is entirely based on a similar concept of 1s and 0s, masculine–feminine balance expressed in the *I Ching* through symbols of solid and broken lines: on/off.

This point is central to bridging scientific knowledge with other branches of knowledge, including archetypal psychology and spiritual traditions. HRV is represented by numbers that reflect the rhythm of the heart. As the master of *Kundalini* yoga, Yogi Bhajan, once said: "Every beat of your heart is the rhythm of your soul."[128] With practice, meditators using HRV feedback can follow the rhythm of their hearts into their souls as they obtain deeper levels of awareness. (Yogi Bhajan also said that "Every beat of your heart is the rhythm of your soul. The voice of your soul is your breath," a concept that will be explicated in Chapter Nine.) HRV offers a mathematics of soul that believers and nonbelievers alike can use, particularly in the study of sine waves.

Sine Wave Patterns in Nature

If you were to trace the circumference of a circle, it would plot out to a sine wave. As the radius reaches 12 noon you are at the top of the sine wave, 3 and 9 are at the center point, and 6 o'clock is the trough of the curve, as shown in Figure 29.

Figure 29 Sine Wave of the Circle. Image credit: Public Domain.[129]

---

128   Harbhajan Singh Khalsa (1929 –2004) introduced *Kundalini* yoga to the West in the late 1960s.
129   https://commons.wikimedia.org/wiki/File:Circle_cos_sin.gif#/media/File:Circle_cos_sin.gif

Anyone who has ever looked at a tide chart recognizes that the semidiurnal tides of the oceans express rhythmic coherence in sine waves. Tidal patterns caused by the dynamic rhythms of the sun and moon are coherent, highly ordered, and yet aperiodic. Just like the heart, the ocean is not a metronome. Fluctuations in timing or heights of the tides do not mask the underlying order to the overall pattern. The peak of each curve in Figure 30 represents high tide, while the bottom of the valley is low tide.

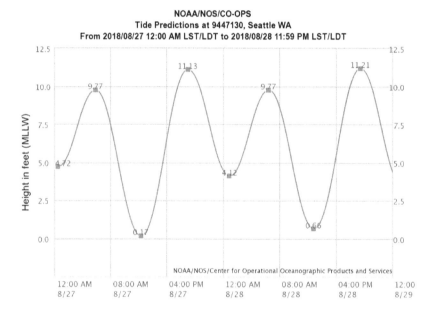

Figure 30 High and Low Tides Over Two Days. Image credit: Courtesy of Noah.[130]

Figure 31 depicts the tides over four weeks in the Puget Sound region, demonstrating the overall coherence of tidal action.

---

130   https://tidesandcurrents.noaa.gov/noaatidepredictions.html?id=9447130 &units=standard&bdate=20180827&edate=20180828&timezone=LST/LDT& clock=12hour&datum=MLLW&interval=hilo&action=dailychart

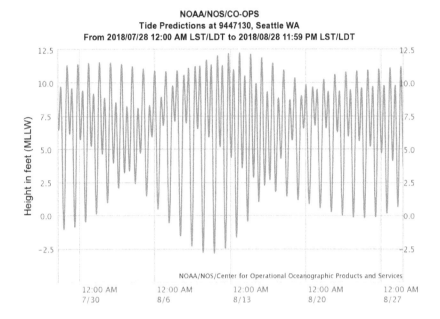

Figure 31 Long-Range Order and Coherence of Tides.
Image credit: Courtesy Noah.[131]

Expanding the time to approximately one month, one sees sine wave patterns within larger patterns. There is a buildup and a winding down to the tidal patterns, correlating to the cycles of the moon. It is amazing to witness the layers of order and coherence in the tidal patterns over time, patterns within patterns. Our hearts are designed to do the same. It is difficult to imagine the chaos that would ensue if the tidal sinusoidal pattern became disrupted for even a short time.

Humans experience stress, anxiety, and depression when the rhythms get out of sync. What are the long-term implications for chronic stress and low heart rhythm coherence, and what impact is this having globally? Such questions are worth considering.

---

131   https://tidesandcurrents.noaa.gov/noaatidepredictions.html?id=9447130&units
=standard&bdate=20180728&edate=20180828&timezone=LST/LDT&clock=12
hour&datum=MLLW&interval=hilo&action=dailychart

CHAPTER SEVEN

Spiral Archetypes, Spiral Universe

*"Progress has not followed a straight ascending line,
but a spiral with rhythms of progress
and retrogression, of evolution and dissolution."*
— Johann Wolfgang von Goethe

Looking at the last figure in Chapter Six, you may also have noticed a kind of spiral. Spiral formations are all around us in nature. As with all archetypal symbols, there is an inexhaustible well of meaning.

The Archetypal Spiral

Like numbers, the union of masculine and feminine spirals and pulsates through the universe, traversing psyche and matter. The tradition of Tantric Shaivism refers to this as *spanda*, the throb of universal consciousness emanating through the cosmos, appearing as spiral and undulating patterns.

From the triple spirals (triskelion or triskele) of the ancient Celts (i.e., New Grange), and reciprocal spirals motif from Malta (Tarxien[132]), to the spirals we have recently seen in the outer reaches of space through photographs from the Hubbell satellite, spirals have existed in psyche and nature since time immemorial. The spiral can be seen in galaxies, seashells, and the pattern of a falcon's dive—and in the

---

132   Spiral motif from Tarxien, https://grahamhancock.com/reedijkl1/

helical structure of our very DNA. Spirals have been primary Goddess symbols since the late Paleolithic. In the Tantric tradition of Hinduism, the spiraling serpent power is known as *kundalini*; in the Christian mythos, the serpent was deemed to be responsible for Adam and Eve's fall from the unitive state.

At one time we believed that the sun and planets rotated around the Earth. Although others, like Aristarchus of Samos, had argued from the fourth century B.C.E. on that the Earth rotates around the sun, the accepted view promulgated by the Catholic Church was that the Earth is at the center of the universe. Then Nicolaus Copernicus revived the heliocentric theory in the 16th century, stating the sun that remains at rest near the center of the universe and that the Earth, spinning on its axis once daily, revolves annually around the sun based on the argument that mathematics should be the basis for such theories.

Modern astronomy has now revealed that the sun itself is moving along with the rest of the solar system and galaxies throughout the cosmos. Pierre Teilhard speculated that everything in the universe is spiraling toward its fated point of singularity (the Omega Point), drawing humanity toward Christ. His notion was of a physio-spiritual spiraling process eventually bringing humanity into coherence with absolute consciousness, or in Teilhard's words, Christ consciousness.

Jung contended that process of individuation and the movement of psyche was also spiral in nature. He wrote:

> We can hardly escape the feeling that the unconscious process moves spiral-wise round a centre, gradually getting closer, while the characteristics of the centre grow more and more distinct. Or perhaps we could put it the other way round and say that the centre—itself virtually unknowable—acts like a magnet on the disparate materials and processes of the unconscious and gradually captures them as in a crystal lattice.[133]

---

133   Psychology and Alchemy (par. 325)

Universal archetypal spiral images are based on the Golden Mean (also called the golden ratio or divine ratio, or the golden section), a concept first described by Pythagoras about 600 B.C.E. and shown in Figure 32. Pythagoras summarized it as a series of relationships in which "the small is to the large as the large is to the whole." Plato considered the Golden Mean to be the most binding of all mathematical relationships and the key to the physics of the cosmos.

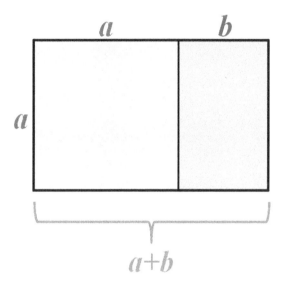

Figure 32 The Golden Mean Rectangle. Image Source: Public Domain.

At the beginning of the Renaissance, Fibonacci, an Italian mathematician, described such patterns as logarithmic spirals. He came up with the Fibonacci Sequence, a highly coherent unfolding of numbers in a spiraling pattern based on the Golden Mean. In the Fibonacci Sequence of numbers, each number is the sum of the previous two numbers, thus: 1, 1, 2, 3, 5, 8, 13, 21, and so on. Visually, this sequence is expressed as a spiral, as shown in Figure 33.

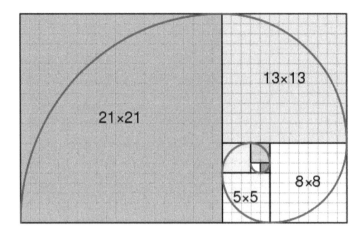

Figure 33 Fibonacci Sequence Expressed as a Spiral.
Image credit: Jahobr, CC0, via Wikimedia Commons.

The Golden Mean is aesthetically pleasing in nature, architecture, and art. It is also desirable on the functional level. We see it at work in the heartbeat. Michael Y. Henein and his coworkers have concluded that "the overall cardiac and ventricular dimensions in a normal heart are consistent with the golden ration and angle, representing optimum pump structure and function efficiency, whereas there is significant deviation in the disease state."[134] The spiral geometry of the anatomical heart is necessary for health, represented in as the spiral HRV footprint that it leaves. The physical and psychological dynamics of the heart are mutually dependent on spiral formations. Incoherent heart rhythms cause chaotic blood flow patterns, creating discord in the heart's muscle pattern.

---

134   Henein, M. Y., Zhao, Y., Nicoll, R., Sun, L., Khir, A. W., Franklin, K., & Lindqvist, P. (2011). The human heart: Application of the golden ratio and angle. *International Journal of Cardiology*, 150(3), 239–242. https://doi.org/10.1016/J.IJCARD.2011.05.094

When natural spiral rhythms lose their integrity, even nature gets off course. Cardiologist Dr. Gerald D. Buckburg draws our attention to other examples in nature that utilize harmony of the whole in relation to the parts, stating, "Spirals are almost the master plan of nature in terms of structure and rhythm."

Spirals are central to many spiritual or wisdom traditions. For many, spirals and spiral movements are the signature of the Creatrix of the universe, which is feminine in form and function. But it is not just spiritual thinkers who see the unitive center of the spiral as a single point, which occupies no space. Quantum physicist and neuroscientist David Bohm wrote:

> . . . each part of space contains waves from everything, which enfold the whole room, the whole universe, the whole of everything. In the implicate order everything is thus internally related to everything, everything contains everything, and only in the explicate order are things separate and relatively independent.[135]

As noted philosopher Ken Wilber expresses through his Integral Theory, every tradition, including mathematics-based science, eventually comes to the realization that the universe is a single coherent whole.[136] Wilber's theory is what Jung popularized as the *unus mundus* (Latin for "one world") one reality underlying everything.

To modern science, the spiral as *unus mundus* is an archetype of coherence; to the ancients, the spiral was the archetype expressing feminine creative power. The underlying archetypal crystalline structure is the spiral and expresses itself as distinct images as discussed earlier in this chapter. One expression is geometric, sine wave; the other is mythical, the snake.

---

135   Bohm, David. *On Creativity*. New York: Routledge. (1996) p. 129.
136   Wilber, Ken. *A Theory of Everything*.

The Sacred Snake

Ancient cultures frequently associated the spiral with serpents or snakes. From the Sumerians and Egyptians to the biblical Eve, the serpent and the feminine are closely linked.

Figure 34 Minoan Snake Goddess figurines, c. 1600 BCE, Archaeological Museum, Heraklion, Crete. Image Credit: Creative Commons.

Found in ancient China, India, and Greece, the caduceus with its twin snakes coiled three times around a central axis provides an archetypal example of the juxtaposition between primal masculine and feminine forces within psyche-soma and the potential for healing and evolution when these two forces are in balanced.

Figure 35 Fuxi and Nüwa. Image Credit: Wiki File:Anonymous-Fuxi and Nüwa.jpg|thumb|Anonymous-Fuxi and Nüwa.

Christian mythology also incorporates the male-female-snake motif depicted as Adam and Eve along with the snake spiraling up an archetypal central axis, as seen at the statue of Madonna with Child in Notre-Dame in Paris, France (Figure 36). The contemporary medical symbol of the caduceus depicts two snakes symmetrically intertwined around a central winged staff, or Hermes's wand.

Figure 36 The story of the Eden Garden. The temptation of Adam & Eve. Pedestal of the statue of Madonna with Child, Western portal (of the Virgin), of Notre-Dame de Paris, France. Image credit: Jebulon, CC0, via Wikimedia Commons.

Mythic representations of complex analogies allow a clearer understanding of the relationship between the nervous system and the masculine and feminine within. Coil means "to gather together."[137] A coil has inherent latent energy, which until stretched or squeezed, lies dormant.

Canadian anthropologist Jeremy Narby pointed out that the Aztec word *coatl* translates to both "serpent" and "twin" and speculated that Quetzalcoatl, the plumed serpent, was the embodiment of the "sacred energy of life."[138] Narby made the connection between

---

137   http://www.etymonline.com/index.php?term=coil
138   In The Cosmic Serpent: DNA and the Origins of Knowledge, 1998, p. 62.

Quetzalcoatl symbolism and the archetypal patterns found in cultures worldwide involving twins, creation myths, serpents, ladders, and comic energy sources.

Activating the Archetypal Imagination: Tantric Yantra Meditation Ritual

Rebalancing the Sacred Feminine and Masculine Within

A Tantric yantra is an Eastern meditation and ritual tool that evokes mythic thinking in the individual. A Tantric yantra is typically a tangible geometrical composition of virtually unlimited combinations of a few primal shapes, including the circle-spiral, triangle, and square. Yantras are mandalas in physical form that are used as meditation devices.

The elementary geometric symbols found in a Tantric yantra serve as a pathway between expansion and contraction, systole and diastole, and finite and infinite. This involution and evolutionary movement is the pulse of the universe, and microcosmically equivalent to the human inhalation and exhalation of the breath. The deep, full inhalation is the expanding universe, and the exhalation condenses down again to the *bindu* point, the point at which the infinite or numinous breaks through.

The expansion and contraction is the pulse of life of humans, the universe, and everything in between. The yantra provides a mechanism for integrating conflicting energies, and the Sri yantra is an excellent choice for rebalancing masculine and feminine energies within the mind-body continuum. Symbolic images, irrespective of cultural context, can activate the sacred within a person; this underscores the universality of symbols and their elemental reduction to the sacred. Geometry is inherent in nature; human and cosmos are one. Focusing on the yantra's archetypal images creates a psychic effect and can be thought of as a pilgrimage toward the center, the unknowable mystery of oneself.

Figure 37 Sri Yantra Mandala. Image Credit: Creative Commons.

The Sri Yantra or Shri Chakra from the Hindu tradition[139] is a harmonizing mandala or sacred harmonizing circle. Nine interlocking triangles have an inherent bindu point at the center of the yantra. A few elementary geometric shapes reveal a mythology of creation that can be experienced by meditating with the aid of this yantra.

The downward-facing triangles enclose sacred feminine energy or matter of the cosmic womb—Sophia. The upward pointing masculine triangles serve as her masculine counterpart, and together they harmonize in coherent wholeness.

For the yantra to have its fullest effect, layer a mantra (sacred sound) over the yantra itself. The mantra Om is monadic and symbolic of the entire cosmos. On the surface, this seed mantra may appear simplistic; however, the physical vibrational pattern affects

---

139   Shri Vidya school of Hinduism

humans at the physical (subtle body), psychological, and spiritual levels. "Om is a complete alphabetical yantra in its own right and can be created with the creative spirit, the bindu." (Khanna, Yantra 37)

Directions

Materials
Sri Yantra, Journal, OM audio.

Either use the yantra in this book or search on the internet for the Sri Yantra in the public domain and print it. Also search for the OM mantra on YouTube or preferably, use your own voice. Have a journal (blank pages of paper) and pen nearby.

Position
Sit comfortably with a straight spine either on the floor or on a chair holding the Sri Yantra at a comfortable distance.

Exercise
1. Soften your gaze as you look at the bindu or center of the Sri yantra. Allow yourself to be lulled into a meditative and slightly hypnotic state to open your doors of perception.

2. Begin a slow inhalation through your nose while expanding your awareness from the center of the yantra to the outer rim of the inner circle. As you exhale, reverse the process as you bring your awareness from the circle back to the bindu point.

3. Listen to the OM mantra and allow your meditative state to self-regulate with the sound current.

Continue for 11 minutes, 22 minutes, or 31 minutes

To end
Inhale deeply and exhale completely three times. Turn OM chant off if using audio. Before you get up and move around, journal for five to 30 minutes and just allow whatever comes to mind flow onto your empty pages.

Optional
If you are practicing heart coherence biofeedback, starting a five-minute session prior to journaling is recommended.

Spiritual Traditions and the Heart

CHAPTER EIGHT

Taoism and Heart Coherence

"If you do not study the I Ching you cannot understand medicine at all."

– Sun Si Miao of the Tang Dynasty

When we think of ourselves as separate from nature, separate from Mother Earth and the universe, we set ourselves up for serious consequences. As has been shown in the preceding chapters, we are literally part of the flow of nature, and when we cut ourselves off from nature, we begin the dis-ease process.

Perhaps no civilization understood this concept better than the ancient Chinese, whose spiritual tradition of universal right order and harmony (coherence), the *tao*, is expressed in the *Tao Te Ching* and the *I Ching, The Book of Changes*. First, we return to the sine wave in the cultural dress of the ubiquitous Taoist symbol, the *yin/yang* or *tajitu*, as shown in Figure 38.

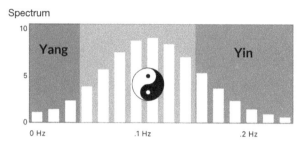

Figure 38 Sympathetic and Parasympathetic Activity Expressed as Yin and Yang, Heart Coherence Expressed as Taijtu. Image credit: Author using HeartMath® Inner Balance and annotated using Canva. Taijtu symbol: Gregory Maxwell, Public domain, via Wikimedia Commons.

The ancient Taoists recognized the dynamic play of the opposites in both psyche and nature. Although the *tajitu* is typically shown in a vertical orientation, if we rotate the symbol (as shown in Figure 39, the sine wave clearly emerges at the interface of the light and dark aspects.

Figure 39 Tajitu Showing Sine Wave Pattern Inherent in Design. Image credit: Gregory Maxwell, Public domain, via Wikimedia Commons.

Each aspect contains the seed of its opposite, showing the interconnectedness of opposite forces. The seed of the light is carried within the dark core, just as the light part contains the opposite dark seed. The positive and negative grow out of each other in a continuous and dynamic flow.

Taoism teaches that the *tajitu* has the capacity to manifest the universe out of the interplay of masculine and feminine forces:

> The Way gave birth to the One
> The One gave birth to the Two
> The Two gave birth to the Three
> And the Three gave birth to the ten thousand things.
> The ten thousand things carry *Yin* on their backs and wrap their arms around *Yang*.
> Through the blending of ch'i they arrive at a state of harmony.[140]

The Way, or *Tao*, is, like an archetype, something that in itself cannot be seen but contains the full potential of the universe. It is the flux at the still center point; it builds, sustains, and pulls apart according to its organizing principles. The *Tao* cannot be pinned down or defined: as Lao-Tzu tells us, the *Tao* that can be named is not the *Tao*. The *Tao* eludes the evidence-based Western paradigm; yet, it is the underlying, ineffable intelligence that holds the universe in a perpetual state of vibrant coherence, of which we are a part. (Here we encounter, once again, the idea of intelligence underlying the mathematical universe.) It is the unseen *Tao* to which one must cohere, but this cannot be done through the rational intellect; rather, one coheres with the *Tao* through the heart. Flowing with the *Tao* is coherent action.

The *I Ching* as a Model of Human-Cosmological Coherence

The scientific mind, *logos*, the masculine voice that speaks the language of reason, logic, and statistics, has muted the feminine voice of wisdom (Sophia), whose native tongue is image, intuition, and deep inner knowing. But as Taoism teaches and as we see at the atomic level of reality, both positive and negative forces are needed to propel

---

140   *Tao Te Ching*, verse 42. Lao-Tzu, a contemporary of Confucius who lived approximately 500 years BCE during the Zhou dynasty, is the recognized author of the *Tao Te Ching*

humans and the universe forward. We can think of these polarities as the archetypal masculine principle and the archetypal feminine principle. These are simply ideas that we traditionally hold in pairs. The universe is not, in fact, gendered; feminine is not equivalent to negative or to the dark. Expressing things in terms of masculine/feminine or positive/negative or young/old is only a tool for working with that which we think of as opposing forces but are in fact necessary to the whole. However, because humans tend to attach more value to one side of an opposition, that which has been called "feminine" has been associated with being negative, being lesser, even being wrong, and that has led to many problems. This book seeks to bring this side of the polarity, which I call Sophia, back into its rightful place as an equal partner in creation.

Fu Hsi, King Wên, the Duke of Chou, and Confucius are credited as the four Holy Sages who compiled and developed the *I Ching* over the course of centuries. In the *I Ching*, the dichotomy between masculine and feminine appears as *yang* and *yin*. A solid line (—) is masculine and broken line (– –) is feminine. The solid line is also referred to as a "closed gate" while the broken line is an "open gate." The *I Ching* uses hexagrams, stacks of six lines, to represent various states of masculine-feminine balance, shown in Figure 40.[141]

In Taoism, the eternal interplay of masculine-feminine opposites is the archetypal basis for all of creation. *Chi'en*, heaven or Spirit, represented by three unbroken lines, is the maximum flow of the creative masculine principle, *yang*. *K'un*, the receptive feminine Earth, is indicated by three broken lines and represents the dark, yielding, receptive primal power of *yin*. Chi'en and K'un have offspring, three sons and three daughters, represented by eight trigrams that are a blend of unbroken and broken lines. Their trigrams are the Abyss, Mountain, Fire, Lake, Wind, and Thunder and Lightning. They stand for principles of change or transformation.[142]

---

141   Perkins, Franklin. *Leibniz and China: A Commerce of Light.* Cambridge: Cambridge UP, 2004. 117. https://commons.wikimedia.org/w/index.php?curid=36231359
142   Govinda, p. 42.

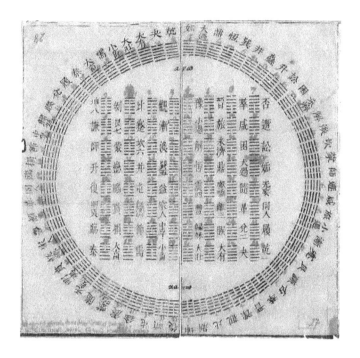

Figure 40 I Ching in Diagram Belonging to Gottfried Wilhelm.
Image credit: Public Domain.

There are 64 possible combinations or hexagrams, which represent the essential building blocks of the universe—just as our DNA is made up of 64 codons.[143] Richard Wilhelm wrote that "the linear images [hexagrams] completely contain the world, they are its embodiment."[144] The hexagrams demonstrate the movement of *yang* and *yin*; like the tide, when the sea reaches its maximum high tide, it becomes full (*yang*), and the energy begins to recede, to turn into its opposite, *yin*. Each hexagram ages or ripens into its opposite and a new cycle begins. The eternal rhythmic flow between *yang* and *yin* reflects the coherent action of the cosmos.

---

143   Narby, Jeremy. *Cosmic Serpent.*
144   *Understanding the I Ching.*

Once a system is in a coherent state, it tends to remain in coherence until something disturbs the equilibrium. Humans knock themselves out of a state of heart coherence primarily through the egoic mind, which pulls one out of higher vibrational frequencies of the Self (states such as compassion, love, peace) and into lower states (such as fear, anxiety, and resentment).

The natural coherent flow of the universe was once accepted by Wisdom traditions as self-evident. Such assertions may seem far-fetched or be immediately discounted by those of a "rational" mindset. However, the wisdom of the *I Ching* aligns with Western science in ways that may not be obvious at the surface level.

For instance, Joachim Bovet, a French Jesuit and sinologist,[145] observed a striking correlation between the numerical underpinnings of the *I Ching* and the binary arithmetic system developed by Bovet's contemporary, Gottfried Leibniz. Leibniz is credited, along with Isaac Newton, for the independent discovery of calculus, which underlies modern mathematics and the sciences.[146] In a letter to Leibniz, Bovet suggested that Christian missionaries should study the *I Ching* in order to frame it as a "science of China" similar to Western mathematics, with the goal of converting the Chinese to Christianity.[147]

Leibniz responded by theorizing that the system of the *I Ching* had value beyond mathematics; he thought that a common harmony underlies mathematics and spiritual truths, and this can be learned through the contemplation of number. In Leibniz's system, the number one (1) represents creative unity (*yang*) and zero (0) stands for chaos (*yin,* or feminine force). In our digital age, the world runs on 1s and 0s as computer code uses only these two values.

---

145   1656-1730

146   Certainly, there are precursory thinkers, including Archimedes, who contributed to the discovery of calculus. Readers interesting in pursing the history of mathematics may find *The History of Mathematics: A Reader* (Gray, 1987) a helpful primer.

147   Translated letters: https://leibniz-bouvet.swarthmore.edu/?s=binary. Interested readers are encouraged to read "The Pre-Established Harmony between Leibniz and Chinese Thought (Cook, 1981)" and "Bovet and Leibnitz: A Scholarly Correspondence" (Swiderski, 1980).

The *I Ching* and Leibniz's system tap into the collective archetypal pool. Both are based on the notion of a preexisting harmony that can be expressed as opposites flowing into each other. The East and the West, Orient and Occident, may have expressed these ideas differently, but underneath they are the same.

The religious scholar and philosopher Joseph Needleman[148] once asked a Taoist monk, Chang Yeh-Yuan, "what is really the fundamental idea of the *Book of Changes*?" The monk responded, "Resonance." Resonance and coherence are interrelated. Coherence relates to a contained system, such as the human body, while resonance refers to two or more systems interacting with each other.

The Transcendent Function

Contrasting Leibniz's binary mathematical system with that of the *I Ching* reflects the dichotomy between science and religion. We can see this as well in the post-Enlightenment, Western scientific perspective on evolution versus that of the Catholic Church prior to Pope Benedict XVI, who held the papacy from 2005 to 2013. Both sides viewed creation in a way that excluded the other. Such a hardline separatism or duality represents what Jung called "the tension of the opposites." It appears that no reconciliation is possible. But the tension can begin to break if a third, higher or "transcendent" viewpoint is brought forth. The idea of the dialectic, in which thesis is opposed by antithesis, then resolved into synthesis, was first posited by German philosopher Johann Fichte at the end of the 18th century.[149]

A century later, Pierre Teilhard de Chardin, a controversial Jesuit priest, philosopher, paleontologist, and geologist (see Chapter Eleven) recognized this process at work in the seeming dichotomy of science and religion. The Church banned his books that sought to reconcile

---

148   http://www.jacobneedleman.com/about/ (Needham, 1956, p. 304).
149   But is usually, and erroneously, credited to G.W.F. Hegel and called the Hegelian dialectic.

the evolutionary theory of nature with Christianity. Teilhard de Chardin compared the Church's view of Christ to that of a child and predicted that as Christianity matured, its consciousness concerning Christ would develop as well, using the analogy of how we understand the sun quite differently from the way our forefathers did.[150] Teilhard de Chardin believed in what he called the "Omega Point," a single point of maximum complexity and consciousness toward which the universe is evolving.

Evolution of consciousness is required to move from a sense of science and religion as polar opposites and instead allow a wholly new solution to emerge. Jung called this process the "union of the opposites" and said that the third, unexpected answer comes about through what he called the transcendent function. The transcendent function moves consciousness forward. If we can sit in the gulf between the opposites and maintain the tension, as Jung suggested, then the transcendent function may gift us with a new paradigm of thought, an option heretofore not considered.

Science maintains that evidence-based methodology, based on logic and reason, is the only viable model for healing. A purely spiritual perspective claims that knowledge of the heart is the central path to healing. HRV can provide an opening for the transcendent function to operate between science and spirituality because both share number symbolism as a common denominator. In Western terms, heart coherence is expressed in numerical form, as we have seen. Similarly, Wisdom traditions have used numbers since time immemorial to express ineffable spiritual concepts, as we discussed in the *I Ching*[151]. In 1955, Jung wrote to Nobel Prize winning physicist Wolfgang Pauli, "My feeling is that the common ground shared by physics and psychology does not lie in the parallelism of the formation of concepts but rather in 'the ancient spiritual dynamis' of number."[152] Jung pulls in not just science and spirituality but also psychology, the

---

150   Chardin P. T., 1976, p. 117.
151   1's and 0's serving as the probable precursor to modern calculus.
152   qtd *Pauli and Jung* 202 //C. A. Meier, ed., Wofgang Pauli und C. G. Jung: Ein Briefwechsel, 1932-1958.

three threads exemplified throughout this book. Number as arche-type weaves through all of creation, from the rotation of an electron around its nucleus to the gravitational forces that dictate order and harmony within the universe, and heart coherence. In Jungian terms, the underlying unity was referred to as *unus mundus,* an underlying unitive order to the cosmos.

EXPERIENTIAL PRACTICE

Transcendent Function:
The Reconciliation of the Opposites

"There is no consciousness without discrimination of opposites" — **(Jung *CW* 9i, par. 1778).**

Heart Coherence is a somatic expression of the transcendent func-tion; it creates self-regulation of the psyche through the two polar opposite forces of the ANS.

Heart Coherence is the transcendent function of the ANS; it is the higher and synergistic expression of the polar dualities of the sympathetic and parasympathetic branches of the ANS.

The masculine-oriented sympathetic branch and its feminine polar opposite reside in the parasympathetic branch. The sympathet-ic-parasympathetic pair are like the gas pedal and brake pedal in your car. They are not designed to be used at the same time. Similarly, your sympathetic and parasympathetic branches are meant to alternate functions; they are not designed to work simultaneously. When in proper balance, the sympathetic branch causes a rise in heart rate, and the parasympathetic is responsible for the slowing of heart rate; gas pedal and brake.

To Begin
Using a HeartMath® Inner Balance device (if available), allow your-self to settle into a state of high heart coherence. Observe the sine wave forming as your heart rate slowing increases as you inhale

and decreases as you exhale. If you do not have an Inner Balance device, then come into a quiet meditative state and follow your breath for several minutes.

Next, recall a time in your life when you experienced a difficult situation that seemed to have no resolution, a time when things appeared truly black and white. You felt like you were between a "rock and a hard place." Then suddenly, almost out of the blue, a new solution came to you spontaneously, perhaps through a remarkable synchronicity, dream, or other unexpected event.

Journal about your experience for 20 minutes or longer. Work to bring back the vivid details and emotional responses to the newly arrived solution. What frustrations did you experience while in the midst of the issue or crisis? How did the resolution come to you?

CHAPTER NINE

Kundalini Yoga: The Science of the Soul and Path to High Heart Coherence

"The divine power, Kundalini, shines like the stem of a young lotus; like a snake, coiled round upon herself, she holds her tail in her mouth and lies resting half asleep as the base of the body."
— **Yoga Kundalini Upanishad (1.82)**

Although sometimes associated with the Sikh religion, *Kundalini* yoga itself is not a religion and is successfully practiced by agnostics and people of other faiths. Yoga means union with the infinite or divine, or the heart of the cosmos. *Kundalini* is the creative energy of consciousness and evolutionary potential that sleeps at the base of the spine, in the area of the sacrum. Yogis teach that it is the energy of the soul itself, the embodied divine Feminine.

Kundalini derives from the Sanskrit word *kundal*, which means the "coil of the lock of the beloved's hair." *Kundal* implies an intimacy between lover and beloved, the masculine and feminine bonding that is possible *within*. The beloved "other" within, the Self, patiently awaits discovery, a concept also found in depth psychology. *Kundal* also contains the notion of "coil," a series of connecting spirals formed by gathering or winding, as discussed in Chapter Six.[153]

---

153   http://www.thefreedictionary.com/coil

Finally, *kundalini* has been associated with the Hindu symbolic equivalent of Christ consciousness. As Christ consciousness is open to all, so is *kundalini* energy.

Followers of *Kundalini* yoga (and other Eastern traditions) believe that *kundalini* permeates the energy of the Earth and the cosmos. The tradition teaches that all physical reality consists of vibrational energies enmeshed in a complex matrix where physical solids vibrate more slowly than mental processes, and both vibrate more slowly than cosmic consciousness, also known as *spanda*, the throb of creation. Paul E. Muller-Ortega, academic scholar of Indian Religion and Hindu Tantra, describes a spectrum of energies where "the infinitely fast vibration of the supreme systematically coalesces and condenses into progressively slower and thicker vibrations, tangible, perceptible forms emerge from the void and formlessness of the ultimate consciousness."[154]

Kundalini master Yogi Bhajan urged students to "use your mind to synchronize your own magnetic field with the cosmic magnetic field, which has a complete interconnection with all other humans, other existences, and realms of material existence."[155] *Kundalini* yoga is a pragmatic spiritual science especially suited for our changing times. Specific *Kundalini* meditations are targeted to stimulate the vagus nerve and balance the *nadis* (subtle energy channels)[156] and ANS. Some *kundalini* meditations target "cold depression," a phenomenon resulting from stress and information overload, while others build resilience.

With regular meditation practice, you can improve your own heart coherence. As you resonate—literally—with stronger magnetic fields within the cosmos, you will not only optimize your HRV numbers, but you may also begin to experience life differently.

Kundalini energy lies dormant at the base of the spine until awakened, usually through conscious spiritual discipline. But for

---

154   *The Yoga of Vibration and Divine Pulsation*, Singh, p. xviii
155   The Mind: Its projections and multiple facets, 1998, p. 8
156   Western instruments are not able to detect the *nadis*—at least not yet.

some people, the awakening is spontaneous, intense, and disruptive. It is imperative that one strengthen and develop the nervous system to be able to withstand the increased "wattage" of spiritual energy.[157] My own personal experience of *kundalini* energy awakening occurred after a full day of *pranayama* practice. I felt a sensation beginning at the base of the spine. The image that came was of mercury rising in an old-fashioned glass thermometer; my spine was the thermometer, and a viscous substance was expanding and rising up my spine. Although there was no discomfort, it was frightening. But because I was trained and experienced in *Kundalini* yoga, I understood what was happening within my body and remained calm. I felt no ill effects during or after this experience, and I will never forget it. Subsequent experiences were lighter and quicker, like a dancing cool flame shooting up my spine.

Such an experience would not be detected by an X-ray or blood work. It is conceivable that different areas of the brain might be seen to light up through neuroimaging, like a PET scan. However, as these experiences are relatively rare, it is unlikely that one could arrange to be scanned at the height of a *kundalini* experience.

Heretofore, the techniques of *Kundalini* yoga had only been transmitted from teacher to individual student. As with many ancient teachings and sacred texts that have lately emerged from hidden sources, the technology for awakening consciousness is now freely available to anyone who desires it. *Kundalini* yoga is just one example of a spiritual practice that enhances and optimizes heart coherence. The Tibetan Buddhist path, esoteric Christianity, Qi Gong, Sufism, Mindfulness and countless other disciplines may be similarly effective in restoring the awakened or coherent heart. As you explore your *cor* values, you can determine the practice that most suitably aligns and resonates with your values. I prefer to use the term *cor* in place of core, because the Latin word *cor* translates to "heart."

---

157 Practitioners interested in *kundalini* energy are encouraged to seek out a certified teacher who is well versed in *kriyas* (exercises), *pranayama* (breath), and *mantra* (sacred sound) done in specific sequences to help modulate the intensified energy for a safe practice.

The Holy Bone and the Chakras

The concept of spiritual energy being concentrated at the base of the spine is not unique to the *Kundalini* Tantric system. The sacrum, a large triangular bone at the base of the spine, is important in several traditions. The word *sacrum* is derived from the Latin, *os sacrum,* meaning "holy bone"; the Greek equivalent, *hieron osteon,* means both "sacred bone" and "sacred temple."[158]

Ancient shamans viewed the sacrum as a portal to other worlds. Archaeologist Brian Stross, Ph.D.,[159] posits that "the sacrum would likely have represented an image of great power, not only in its symbolic control of the passage of energy and entities between worlds or levels of the cosmos, but also because of its ambiguity, its transformational capabilities, and its ability as a symbol to adapt to changing cultural traditions."[160] The origins of the meanings of the sacrum remain unclear, and there is only speculation that it was considered sacred because it served to protect the genitals, used in rituals, and was believed to be the last bone in the body to decay.

While the sacrum was sacred to the ancients, its spiritual significance appears to have atrophied in the West. However, with the rising interest in Eastern spirituality and shamanic traditions over the past several decades, there has been a resurgence of interest in the power held within the sacral area of the body, the resting ground of *kundalini.*

Kundalini, or *Kundalini-Shakti,* is the feminine energy of consciousness, also referred to as the "nerve of the soul," which, before awakening, is coiled three and a half times at the root chakra (*muladhara*) at the base of the spine. Before I discuss chakras, it is

---

158 https://www.google.com/search?q=sacrum&ie=utf-8&oe=utf-8&aq=t&rls =org.mozilla:en-US:official&client=firefox-a&channel=sb#channel=sb&q=sacrum+ etymology&rls=org.mozilla:en-US:official

159 Professor University of California, Berkeley. Interests: Linguistic Anthropology, Indigenous Mesoamerica, Maya Iconography and Epigraphy, Anthropology of Food, Ethnobotany, Cultural Forms.

160 *The Mesoamerican sacrum bone: Doorway to the Otherworld.* http://research. famsi.org/aztlan/uploads/papers/stross-sacrum.pdf bstross@mail.utexas.edu

important to note that *kundalini* has a physiological component to it, although it not something that is measurable using scientific instrumentation, at least not yet. Michael Molina of the Emerging Sciences Foundation effectively captures the elusive nature of *kundalini* when he states that it is: "A biological mechanism in the body responsible for all forms of spiritual experience, including enlightenment. Also responsible for genius and certain forms of insanity.[161]" Molina's definition incorporates all three of *kundalini's* essential phases, 1) physical, 2) psychological, and 3) spiritual.

Returning now to chakras, they are vortices of energy, arranged vertically along the spine, and correspond to the major nerve plexus of the body; they are integral to several Eastern systems of spirituality and medicine.[162] The first three chakras, located at the root (anus), sex organs, and just below the navel, constitute the "lower triangle" of one's baser (that is, egoic or animal) nature. The upper chakras, located at the throat, forehead (third eye), and crown of the head, constitute the "upper triangle" of higher awareness. The heart center, located just above the physical heart, is the balance point between the lower and upper triangles. The heart chakra is the pivot point between spirit and matter, blending masculine and feminine polarities in right relation.

Figure 41 shows the *anahata*, symbol of the heart chakra. It conveys coherence of the masculine and feminine principles through two overlapping triangles. The upward-pointing triangle symbolizes the masculine principle while the downward one represents the feminine. Both primal energies are balanced and resonate with each other and the greater whole.

---

161   "Kundalini: Unlocking the Secrets of Spiritual Awakening." https://youtu.be/y4cApRG0g44

162   Ajit Mookerjee. *Kundalini: The Arousal of the Inner Energy* (Mookerjee, 1982)

Figure 41 Symbol for the Heart Chakra, Anahata. Original Art by Morgan Phoenix. Image credit: Morgan Phoenix, CC BY-SA 3.0 <https://creativecommons.org/licenses/by-sa/3.0>, via Wikimedia Commons.

When the heart chakra is balanced, this level of consciousness allows compassion, kindness, love, and forgiveness to flow through one's psyche and body. Genuine feelings of love and compassion bring one's heart into a high state of coherence.

The Autonomic Nervous System and *Kundalini* Yoga

The Eastern concept of energy pathways, *nadis,* is not the same as the Western idea of the nervous system, yet the two are associated as homologues. One might think of the *nadis* as being one step removed from the nervous system. The *nadis* are aligned with and yet subtler than the physical nervous system.

The three primary *nadis* are the *pingala* (masculine, or Shiva principle), *ida* (feminine, or Shakti principle), and *sushmana* (neutral). There are thousands of *nadis*; however, *Kundalini* yoga teaches that as the yogi masters the three primary *nadis* through disciplined spiritual practice, the rest will adjust naturally. Originating at the base of the spine, the *pingala nadi* dominates the right side of the body and terminates at the right nostril. Its energy evokes the masculine principle: sun, heat, and projective energy, and represents a positive charge. The *pingala nadi* correlates to the sympathetic branch of the ANS.

The "fight or flight" response of the sympathetic branch is imagined as the thunderbolt of Shiva.

Ida characteristics include eliminating, cooling, calming, imaginative, lunar energy, and receptive. The *ida nadi* traverses the left side of the body from the base of the spine to the left nostril. The *ida nadi* correlates the parasympathetic branch of the ANS. When Shiva dominates the dance, Shakti becomes overwhelmed.

Like the caduceus, *pingala* and *ida* are usually depicted as twin snakes coiled around the *sushmana*. Where the *pingala* and *ida nadis* intersect, a chakra, or energy vortex, emerges. According to the *Mundaka Upanishad 2.6*, "Where all the nerves meet like spokes in a wheel/There he dwells, the One behind the many." *Kundalini* is the emanation both of the soul and the energy of the whole cosmos, which flows through every human to one degree or another. When the flow increases, so does the potential for awareness.

Figure 42 Modern Depiction of the Caduceus.
Image Credit: Public Domain.

Yoga practitioners learn to uncoil the energy stored and direct it to the crown chakra at the crown of the head. When this happens, a new sensitivity opens, and expanded clarity ensues. For example, people have reported a sudden understanding of sacred texts that were previously unintelligible (see Appendix, Lillian's Case Study). The channel of the soul opens, and self-realization becomes a reality.

Jung and *Kundalini,* and the Feminine Voice of Individuation

Jung wrote *The Psychology of Kundalini Yoga* as an explication of four lectures that he delivered to the Psychological Club in Zurich in 1932, expounding on his psychological interpretation of *Kundalini* yoga. A theme common to wisdom traditions and Jungian thought is the necessary realignment of one's ego with the Self (the Beloved in Sufism, the Atman in Hinduism, the Inner Christ in Christianity). Jung sought parallels between the Indian chakra system and depth psychology as he built a model of the progression of higher stages of consciousness.

Kundalini energy, with her powerful feminine presence and allure, draws us into adventures that we might not otherwise pursue. She is a *daimon* like Plato's Diotima, a feminine essence that guides and directs us on our path through the dark woods (as Dante expresses it in *The Divine Comedy*) as we move toward individuation, or self-realization, union with the infinite. Jung referred to the psychological drive to individuate as "the *Kundalini,*" an ineffable quality within the human psyche that draws us beyond the limitations of our egoic will and onto our unique transformation path, when he wrote:

You see, the Kundalini in psychological terms is that which makes you go on the greatest adventures. I say, 'Oh, damn, why did I ever try such a thing? But if I turn back, then the whole adventure goes out of my life, and my life is nothing any longer; it has lost its flavor.' It is this quest that makes life livable, and this is Kundalini; this is the divine urge.[163]

To refuse the call to adventure is to return to the wasteland, a life devoid of meaning. To take the known path and resist the beckoning soul creates a *senexed* heart: one that is prematurely hardened, congealed, and old.[164] A *senexed* heart is a betrayal of psyche or soul; it separates us from creativity's eternal wellspring. The call to

---

163   *The Psychology of Kundalini Yoga,* 1996, p. 21.
164   *Senex* comes from the Latin for old man or woman. Words such as senator, senior, and Saturn are derived from senex and indicate wisdom; however, too much of the Senex archetype results in excessive inflexibility and lack of youthful creativity.

individuate is a mysterious force that seduces one into the forest where there is no path set before us.

But who or what is really calling us? Hillman, as discussed in Chapter Eight, called it our acorn, our soul's purpose. Jung saw it as an impulse to individuate, to become our true unique self—but also to unite our finite self with something greater than ourselves, the infinite. By understanding the nature and potency of *kundalini,* we call forth the internal feminine, or *anima,* and move toward individuation, for as Jung proclaimed, "the anima is the *Kundalini* [. . .] the sleeping beauty."[165]

Jungian psychology teaches that men internally carry the *anima* as their "inner feminine," whereas women carry the contrasexual notion of the *animus.* We are wise not to corner Jung in literalism; rather, reimagine the *anima,* or Shakti, as the Divine Feminine, available to all beyond the boundaries of gender segregation. I agree with Hillman's view that *anima* and *animus* are two aspects of one archetype. Men, women, and the Earth are individuating (although perhaps not all at once), becoming who and what we were born to be, and the Divine Feminine is needed more than ever now—which we will explore more fully in Chapter Eleven.

---

165   Jung, The Psychology of Kundalini Yoga, 1996, p. 23.

Twin Serpents Breathing

Inhaling is a homologue of expansion or unfolding. At the top of the breath, or maximum inhalation, there is a subtle pause and the process reverses into exhalation, the enfolding of the universe within. Humans and the field of psyche are enmeshed within the greater cosmos; depending on the degree of one's own coherence, we overlap energy fields or create interference patterns accordingly.

Put another way, developing cardiac coherence reestablishes the balance between the dance of Shiva and Shakti, the positive and negative electromagnetic fields within psyche, soma, and the cosmos. *Swara* yoga, the science of nostril breathing, is dedicated to the practice of consciously breathing through the left (lunar, feminine) and right (sun, masculine) nostrils to affect the flow of vital energy and *prana*, the life energy. The breath follows a spiral pattern, putting one in sync with the spiral energy of the cosmos.

Each breath is an opportunity to surrender the ego to the Self and merge Self with the life force. Practicing this technique consciously expands the life force energy throughout the body and the energy field. One who masters the breath has mastered the life force energy. As one gains experience, there is less need to control the breath and more surrender to and merging *with* the breath.

Heart coherence can be improved almost immediately by simply inhaling slowly and deeply and exhaling in the same manner. Inhalation inhibits the vagal nerve, and heart rate increases, while exhalation activates the vagal nerve, and heart rate slows down. HRV biofeedback training combined with *pranayama* is highly effective in improving/optimizing heart coherence.

To Begin: Basic Breath Series

Part 1. Left Nostril Breathing

Sit in Easy Pose (cross-legged) or in a chair. Rest the left hand in Gyan Mudra (tip of the thumb presses tip of the index finger). The left wrist is on your left knee.

Place your right hand by your right nostril with the palm flat facing to the left. Gently block the right nostril with your thumb as you begin long, deep, diaphragmatic breathing. Breath only through the left nostril. Inhale through the left nostril and exhale through the left nostril.

Time: 1 – 3 minutes.

To end, inhale and suspend breath comfortably for 10-30 seconds. Exhale and relax.

Part 2. Right Nostril Breathing

Now reverse nostrils and continue as directed above, this time inhaling slowly through the right nostril and exhaling slowly through the right.

Time: 1 – 3 minutes.

To end, inhale and suspend breath comfortably for 10-30 seconds. Exhale and relax.

Part 3. Alternate Nostril Breathing

Now begin to inhale through the left nostril while blocking off the right, then exhale through the right while blocking off the left nostril. Keep the breath long, deep, and smooth.

Time: 1 – 3 minutes.

To end, inhale and suspend breath comfortably for 10-30 seconds. Exhale and relax.

Part 4. Alternate Nostril Breathing

Repeat the previous exercise, except reverse nostrils. Inhale through the right nostril and exhale through the left, using the techniques as before.

Continue with long, deep, regular breaths for 1 – 3 minutes.

To end, inhale and suspend breath comfortably for 10-30 seconds. Exhale and relax.

Part 5. Breath of Fire

(Note: not recommended for pregnant women or women on early menstrual cycle)

Begin a powerful, regular, and conscious Breath of Fire by pulling the navel in as you exhale powerfully through the nose, and allow the inhale to occur passively. For a short tutorial on Breath of Fire see: https://youtu.be/Y0sxdW1WkFo

Time: 1-3 minutes.

To end, inhale and suspend breath comfortably for 10-30 seconds. Exhale and relax.

CHAPTER TEN

The Wisdom of the Heart in Other Traditions

"Why are you knocking at every other door?
Go, knock at the door of your own heart."
— Rumi

Other Eastern Wisdom traditions have much to teach us about the heart in both its physical and spiritual dimensions, as does the field of archetypal psychology.

The Wisdom of the Heart in Sufism

As with most religions, Islam offers two complementary paths, one exoteric—based on doctrine and readily understood by the majority of believers—and the other esoteric or mystical. The contemplative esoteric path of Sufism is elusive and individualistic, providing less specific guidance for the seeker or wayfarer. Sufism teaches that it is through one's heart center that one progresses on the spiritual journey. The heart is the organ of perception through which one gains knowledge of the hidden reality. It is purified through spiritual practice or by aesthetic delight, as when captured by the beauty of art and poetry. The Sufi tradition reveres the purified or illumined heart as the "eye" that sees the Divine. The heart serves as the central connection between the finite human (often referred to in Sufi poetry as the lover) and the Infinite, the Beloved.

The 13th-century mystical poet Jalal al-Din Rumi stated that the seeker cannot merely imitate or "go through the motions" of spiritual practice. One must enter into the experience directly. Rumi's poetry provides the map but not the territory. Rumi described the connection between the subtle and gross heart as "a link beyond all description and comparison / between the Lord of creatures and their inner being."[166] Sufism teaches that there is a relationship between subtle and gross realms that appears to be beyond the comprehension of the rational mind. Lack of empirical knowledge does not negate the possibility of *experiencing* the connection between subtle and gross realms. This connection takes place in what Henry Corbin called the imaginal realm.

Corbin expressed the imaginal realm, perceived through the heart as "the limit, which separates and at the same time unites [corporeal and intelligible]." The imaginal is the liminal space that bridges the in-between-ness of ordinary consciousness and that of the spiritual realm. Sufism calls this bridge the *barzakh,* an intermediary between two realms. Chittick defined *Barzakh* as "'isthmus'; the intermediate realm where people are 'located' between death and resurrection; also the World of Imagination, between the World of Spirits and the World of Bodies."[167] The term "isthmus" provides a vivid image that clearly communicates the notion of a thin separation between two powerful forces; a thin strip of land separating two bodies of water, two heartbeats separated by a "flat line" (somatically), or different levels of consciousness symbolically united through a metaphorical mirror.

This bridge, or isthmus, between two disparate entities, one elemental and one spiritual, permeates that which it separates, yet is a distinct third or "other." As with Jung's transcendent function theory, a third entity emerges from two conflicting or polarized forces. Human consciousness and Divine consciousness are separated by the heart, a third entity, which both unites and divides. The intermediate state of *barzakh* describes such a state in the Islamic tradition.

The *imaginal* mirror found in Sufism symbolizes the reflective quality of the heart, the organ by which the seeker sees the Infinite

---

166   Qtd. Seyyed Hossein, Nasr. Islamic Art and Spirituality. New York: SUNY Press, 1987. p. 139.

167   Chittick, William. C. (Ed.) *The Inner Journey: Views from the Islamic Tradition.* Sandpoint, ID: Morning Light, 2007. P. 303.

and the Infinite sees the seeker, and therefore serves as a *barzakh*. Corbin defined *barzakh* as "an interworld, limiting and conjoining time and eternity, space and transpace [. . .] the conjunction of the sensory and the intelligible in the pure space of the archetype—Images."[168] The heart has access to wisdom beyond the bounds of time and space—in the realm of intuition and creativity.

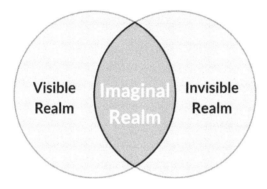

Figure 43 Vesica Piscis Circles. Image credit: Creative Commons; Text: Author.

Figure 44 Dream Image of Human and Angel inside Vesica piscis, Image Credit: Lillian.

---

168   Corbin, Henry. *Spiritual Body and Celestial Earth: From Mazdean Iran to Shī'ite Iran*. Princeton, NJ: Princeton UP, 1977. P. 80.

In her essay on the Sufi poet Hafiz, the English explorer and dip-lomat Gertrude Bell writes, "The Sufi path is necessarily experiential, and it is possible today for someone to draw upon Sufi philosophy and be a participant in another religious tradition."[169] As with *Kundalini* yoga, one does not need to be a believer in a religious tradition in order to receive substantial benefit from its practices. Individuals who are not Sufis can still experience an opening of the heart through the engagement with its poetry.

The intellect may prepare one for the recognition of spiritual truths, but until the movement from head to heart happens by sur-rendering ego, there may be no significant psycho-spiritual progress. The ecstatic and inspired poetry of Rumi is designed to entice the lower soul (*nafs*) by the passionate appeal of beauty and harmony (coherence) to transform and reach the higher state of the "pacified heart," or soul.

Sufis teach that by purifying one's heart through contemplation, prayer, and meditation (*dhikr*), one opens the soul to healing and transformation. Spiritual purification illuminates the heart, generat-ing *himma*, the creative power of the heart. Henry Corbin describes the purpose of *himma* as ". . . the concentration of the heart as the organ which makes it possible to achieve the true knowledge of things, a knowledge inaccessible to the intellect."[170] *Himma* is the heart's longing; when present, *himma* makes the imaginal real. It is the intangible quality of the subtle heart that brings images to life and allows their symbolism to unfold. Corbin described *himma* as equivalent to "the Greek word *enthymesis*, which signifies the act of meditating, conceiving, imagining, projecting, ardently desiring."[171] *Himma* can be thought of as the creative power of the heart.

For Sufis, spiritual practices "polish the mirror" of the heart, cleansing the heart of impurities that veil one from the Beloved or

---

169   *Hafiz, the Mythic Poets.* Trans. Gertrude Bell. Skylight Paths Publishing: Woodstock, VT, 2004. P. 34.

170   Corbin, Henry. *Alone with the Alone: Creative Imagination in the Sufism of Ibn ʿArabi.* Princeton: Princeton UP, 1997. P 229.

171   In his analysis of the works of Ibn ʿArabi, *Creative Imagination* 224.

God. Likewise, Eastern Christian Orthodox thinking refers to a "cloud" that obscures God from the seeker.[172] In Patanajali's *Yoga Sutras*[173], one of the oldest yogic texts, such impurities are called *kleshas*.[174] They obscure the inner *atman*, or divine self, from *Brahman*, the universal consciousness of which *atman* is a part.

The metaphors of the dusty mirror and the cloud refer to mental states that cloud the mind. Sufis and Orthodox Christians believe that the continual remembrance of God through prayer cleanses the mirror, pierces the cloud of unknowing. Prayer is not an intellectual endeavor; rather, heartfelt prayer changes the vibrational frequency of the practitioner. Christian mystic Cynthia Bourgeault describes it as a "homing frequency" to which one can continually fine-tune oneself.[175]

The Eastern Orthodox Church centered in Constantinople and the Roman Catholic Church (Rome) became two distinct and separate branches of Christianity as a result of the East-West Schism (or Great Schism) of 1054. While both traditions mention the importance of the heart, the Eastern Orthodox tradition places a central importance on the role of the heart (Greek: *kardia*). The Eastern Orthodox tradition teaches that the heart has a threefold nature: the physical organ, soul/psyche, and its spiritual aspect, whereupon sacrifice and death, the divine and human is consummated.[176] Theophan the Recluse[177], for example, asserted that the heart is the inner [hu]man and that "the heart is life, and you must live there"[178] and that one must pray with the "mind in the heart".[179] Accordingly, there is oral prayer

---

172　The Cloud of Unknowing

173　The Yoga Sutras are a collection of 196 Indian aphorisms (sutras) on the theory and practice of yoga. Patanjali systematized the central tenets of yoga and organized them in one text, prior to 400 BCE.

174　In Hinduism and Buddhism, *kleshsa* are mental states that cloud the mind causing suffering.

175　The Heart of Centering Prayer, p. 69

176　*Philokalia Vol. 2* 383

177　1815-1894 Theophan contributed to the editing of the *Philokalia*, sacred texts from 4th and 15th centuries. He was canonized by the Russian Orthodox Church in 1988.

178　*The Art of Prayer: An Orthodox Anthology.* Faber and Faber. 1966. P. 184

179　*ibid* P. 276

(bodily), prayer of the mind, and prayer of the heart[180] used to purify the heart.

The purified heart produces psycho-spiritual coherence with the Divine or cosmos. Multiplicity becomes unity. Corbin described "[. . .] the heart as the organ which makes it possible to achieve the true knowledge of things, a knowledge inaccessible to the intellect."[181]

When the heart is in a state of physiological coherence, as discussed in Chapter Two, it creates a strong energetic field that meshes with the greater fields of the Earth and cosmos. From a Sufi perspective, in this state the heart becomes a "mirror" whereby one gains access to a higher plane of reality and encounters the Divine.

The heart sees into subtle realms. Swiss-born Islamic philosopher and 20th-century scholar Frithjof Schuon suggests, "If the Eye of the Heart is generally thought of as being hidden in [hu] man and looking at God [. . .] this same Eye [...] is also—and even above all—the eye of God that looks at man."[182] Schuon also spent considerable time with the Oglala Sioux, where he encountered a similar idea:

The heart is the sanctuary at the center of which is a small space where the Great Spirit (*Wakan Tanka*) lives, and this is the Eye of the Great Spirit by which He sees everything, and with which we see Him. [. . .] (Chante Ognaka, Sioux term for Pocket of his Heart).

Jung and Hillman were both influenced by such concepts, leading to an emphasis in depth psychology on the imaginal heart and its capacity to "see through" or perceive images.

The physiological counterpart of the pure or clean heart is the coherent heart. For the heart to serve as the organ of perception, it must first be in a state of coherence, not just with the energy fields around it but with the values of the person.

---

180 *ibid* P. 21

181 Corbin, Henry. *Alone with the Alone.* 229

182 Schuon, Frithjof. *The Eye of the Heart* 9

Archetypal Psychology and 'Cor' Values

> *"In the City of Brahman is secret dwelling, the Lotus of the Heart. Within this dwelling is a space, and within that space is the fulfillment of our desires. What is within that space should be longed for and realized."*
>
> — Chandogya Upanishad VIII, 1.1.

Heart-brain communication is discussed in Chapter Two from a physiological, evidence- based perspective. The neural network discovered by Armour substantiates what many wisdom traditions understand: that the heart has a "mind of its own" and contains secret or hidden wisdom. Yet the notion that the heart has intelligence and holds secrets unknown to the brain has been largely lost in modern times.

Part of the heart's wisdom is contained in a person's *cor* values, values that are unique and important to a person. Such values may or may not align with family, community, or national values. They are values of the soul. The Hindu text of the *Chandogya Upanishad* teaches that the heart holds the desires that are unique to you and what you ought to be striving toward in life. *Cor* values emanate from one's own heart center, and the more aligned you are with your *cor* values, the more coherent your heart will be physiologically and psychologically. And because our hearts' energy fields interconnect, individual coherence contributes to the field of human coherence.

Cor values may be hidden—secret. It is the job of the seeker to unveil this inner wisdom. The Hindu tradition speaks liberally of the heart holding divine secrets hidden metaphorically in a "cave" or "lotus" as the secret chamber.[183] Christians may prefer to think of the sacred Heart of Christ as symbolizing the cauldron of transformation.

Those who have no interest in spiritual traditions can turn to the work of James Hillman, the founder of archetypal psychology. Hillman illustrates the gist of *cor* values in his acorn theory

---

183   "Hidden in the cave of the heart" (*Katha Upanishad* 2.12) and "Lotus of the heart" Chandogya Upanishad VIII, 1.1.

(or acorn myth, as he preferred to call it).[184] An acorn's destiny is to become a great oak tree, not a cherry or a fir tree. Its DNA is structured that way; its blueprint is set for an oak tree.

Hillman theorized that like the acorn, a person has a predestined life calling and is imprinted onto his or her soul. Plato might have called this concept a *paradigm*. Your acorn is your paradigm or template for being in this world: what you do and how you do it.

Too often we let collective norms define who we are and what we will do in life. How many potentially gifted teachers, poets, or healers have been pushed into more lucrative careers so that they can live in material comfort? My desire for a career in the humanities or psychology was thwarted by a well-meaning mother. (I have no regrets and assume responsibility for my choice to follow her wishes instead of my own.) Earning a bachelor of science degree in medical technology required me to learn calculus, organic chemistry, statistics, and other subjects for which I had sufficient—sometimes barely—talent. I achieved a career, but it was not my vocation; it was not based on my *cor* values. Finding the doorway out of the clinical chemistry world and on to my true calling, to realign with my acorn, took decades.

The price for taking the path of your soul's calling can be heavy, especially when those close to you do not agree with your choices. However, the consequences of a life *not* aligned with *cor* values is even more devastating. Such a life carries a silent stress that many keep at bay through addictive behaviors or other forms of numbing. Yet, it secretly gnaws away at your soul. The development of the acorn into the oak tree is thwarted as long as it continues to try to be what it is not. The poet masquerades as an engineer or gifted artists work for a corporation whose values are abhorrent to them. Internal and silent stress induced by living a life based solely on values of materialism induces anxiety, depression, and dis-ease.

Cor values align with and support your personal destiny, your acorn. A vocation is a calling from within, whereas a career is a path

---

184   On Soul, Character and Calling: A Conversation with James Hillman By Scott London http://www.scottlondon.com/interviews/hillman.html

initiated by the ego's wants and fears—where most of your time is spent funneling your life force energy. If you are not in alignment with your inner essence at the *cor* level, you are living with perpetual stress and increased risk of dis-ease.

Hillman posits, "The acorn theory says that there is an individual image that belongs to your soul."[185] Much like the Hindu lotus of the heart or the sacred Heart of Christ, it takes work to find the hidden image held within. In a busy life, the voice of the heart gets buried. We don't hear its subtle callings—until, perhaps, like Jung, we have a major cardiac event that opens us to the wisdom of the heart.

EXPERIENTIAL PRACTICE

Christian Contemplative Centering Prayer

> *"When the field of vision has been unified, the inner being comes to rest, and that inner peaceableness flows into the outer world as harmony and compassion."*
>
> — Cynthia Bourgeault[186]

The method of the Centering Prayer or The Prayer of Consent[187] was born out of Father Thomas Keating's Abby by a group of Trappist Monks in the late 1960s. The now popular Centering Prayer was sourced from the *The Cloud of Unknowing*, an anonymous work of Christian mysticism written in the latter half of the 14th century. From the Eastern Christian tradition, prayer is an art that requires

---

185   2012 Interview on Scott London's website: https://scott.london/interviews/hillman.html

186   *The Wisdom of Jesus: Transforming the Heart and Mind.* Shambhala Publications, Boston: 2008. p46).

187   Thomas Keating's The Method of CENTERING PRAYER THE PRAYER OF CONSENT Guidelines can be found at: https://www.contemplativeoutreach.org/sites/default/files/private/center_prayer_method_2017-01_0.pdf

one primary focus: the consolidation of consciousness in the heart, to stand with the attention in the heart where it can take root (*Art of Prayer* 96).

The Centering Prayer has a key similarity to the yogic science of *pratyahar*— synchronizing yourself to nothingness, the ultimate surrender. The Centering Prayer and *pratyahar* requires that you let go of all thought. To further assist in understanding this concept, the image of a tortoise pulling in all four legs and head may be useful. This symbolizes the withdrawal of the five senses and entering a state of zero, *Shuniya*, from the yogic perspective; and for Christians, it prepares the faculties and readies the practitioner for receiving the gift of contemplation.

The practice of *hesychia*, Greek for stillness, is similarly the withdrawal of the senses from the external world and shifting one's awareness inward with the intention of listening to God (*Philokalia Vol 2* 387).

To stand guard over the heart, to stand with the mind in the heart, to descend from the head to the heart—all these are one and the same thing. The core of the work lies in concentrating the attention and the standing before the invisible Lord, not in the head but in the chest, close to the heart and in the heart. When the divine warmth comes all this will be clear (Palmer, 1966).

The Centering Prayer is intended for the modern believer who is seeking a path grounded in the Christian Contemplative tradition. The concept of the "putting the mind in the heart" is central to The Centering Prayer.

Brief overview of how the method is practiced[188]:

- ♥ Find a quiet place and sit somewhere where you won't be interrupted, if possible.

- ♥ Sit on a meditation cushion, meditation bench, or chair that allows you to keep your spine straight.

---

188   https://wisdomwayofknowing.org/resource-directory/centering-prayer/. Accessed 12-21-19 at 1:34 PST

- ♥ The prescribed daily practice is: two sessions for a minimum of 20 minutes each. Use a timer, if possible, so that you won't be tempted to keep checking the time.

- ♥ Choose a sacred word to your liking, preferably one syllable, such as God, love, or peace. The sacred word is to be used as a symbol or placeholder for your intention of open availability to God and consent for "God's presence and action within."

- ♥ Sit with your eyes closed and relax into a state of awareness.

- ♥ When you notice that you have drifted into thought, distracted by a bodily sensation, or experience some mental focus, silently insert your sacred word and simply let go of your thoughts. Your sacred word is not meant to be continuously chanted like a mantra. Silently and gently introduce your sacred word and return to a state of awareness.

- ♥ At the end of your session, remain in silence with your eyes closed for a couple of minutes.

Further Reading: Cynthia Bourgeault's *The Heart of Centering Prayer: Nondual Christianity in Theory and Practice.* Cynthia Bourgeault provides valuable insights into the Nondual aspects of Christianity through the reading of *The Cloud of Unknowing* and the practice of The Centering Prayer. Bourgeault teaches that by putting the "mind into the heart," we eliminate subject and object and rewire our fields of perception. (https://youtu.be/TufpAQUXpTo 13:10-13:22).

The Cosmic Heart of Sophia

CHAPTER ELEVEN

The Feminine and the Heart

"She visits during dream time
She is the spinner of the spiral flow of blood leaving the heart
She causes you to glance back as she escapes the corner of
your eye
She is the blue in the halo that glistens around the wise one's
head
She lies at the center of the philosopher's stone
She is the evolutionary force of the universe
If you deny Her, you deny life; matter deadens
If you embrace Her in your heart, your soul joins with Hers;
matter becomes spiritualized
She is generative and redemptive, the rhythm of Nature,
moving life forward
She is the tension in the coil of the beloved's hair"[189]

In this chapter, we begin to unveil Sophia, feminine wisdom, so we can tap into the Cosmic Heart. The essential quality of this wisdom, contrasted with masculine *logos*, is communicated succinctly in the words of the Sufi mystic Llewellyn Vaughan-Lee:

> We all have both masculine and feminine qualities. [. . .] Because a woman creates new life from her own body she has an instinctual understanding of the spiritual essence of life. [. . .] A man needs to transmute his instinctual power drive until it is surrendered to the will of God [Universal intelligence].[190]

---

189   poem by the author
190   Vaughan-Lee, 2017, *The Return of the Feminine and the World Soul, 203-204.*

Patriarchal forces that privilege *power over* rather than *power among*—an attitude present within both men *and* women—have dominated Western culture for many centuries, negatively impacting all of humanity. The cosmic heart of Sophia needs to be unveiled, redis-covered so that she can facilitate a rebalancing of healthy masculine and feminine forces, restoring both individual and collective harmony and coherence. Likewise, the problems that imminently threaten our civilization can no longer be solved using *power over* strategies. If, instead, we merge masculine knowledge with feminine wisdom, we can find solutions for healing not just personal heart maladies but also the diseased heart of the world.

As discussed in the prior section, masculine and feminine principles exist not only on the physical plane (male and female in the gender sense), but also on the psychological and subtle planes of reality. When masculine and feminine aspects in all these areas become synchronized, higher states of awareness ensue. Jung referred to this synchronization of masculine and feminine forces as the mystical marriage, the *coniunctionis*.

Although Jung speculated that the nervous system was an inte-gral part of higher consciousness, the medical technologies that could support his hypothesis (such as HRV and brain imaging) were not available during his lifetime. Nonetheless, he foresaw that the nervous system would play a key role in understanding consciousness, intuit-ing that there is "some other nervous substrata in us, apart from the cerebrum, that can think and perceive."[191] He was right.

The degree to which one perceives consciousness appears varied dependent upon psycho-somatic coherence. Said another way, the degree to which Sophia's veil is lifted determines the degree of per-ceived consciousness.

Without sufficient training and practice, most people are incapable of achieving higher states of awareness of their own accord. Reaching such states of awareness is the goal of most Eastern and Indigenous spiritual practices, as well as esoteric Western traditions such as

---

191   *CW* Vol. 8, p 509

Eastern Christian mysticism, the Kabbalah tradition of Judaism, and the ecstatic dances of Sufism.

The *Yoga Sutras* of Patanjali, which dates from 400 B.C.E. or earlier, posits a progressive hierarchy of consciousness that leads to an unveiling of full human consciousness. Patanjali identified eight interrelated aspects of yoga called the Eight-Limbed path,[192] each with its own subclassifications. The limbs work in harmony with one another, and one progresses toward *Samadhi*, the ultimate state of awakening.

Kundalini yoga, *Kriya* yoga, and *Ashtanga* yoga are examples of yoga traditions that follow Patanjali's Eight Limbs. Many Westerners associate yoga only with postures and perhaps meditation and *pranayam*. Yoga is a lifestyle for the serious yoga student, taking yoga practice beyond an exercise class.

The Secret of the Golden Flower, a central text in both the Buddhist and Taoist traditions, outlines how to recognize and attain the various stages of human consciousness that lead to ultimate consciousness.[193] The "golden flower" symbolizes the potential within the human psyche that can be made available through rigorous spiritual practice. The golden flower is a feminine symbol whose petals unfurl to reveal the inner light of consciousness. Like the veiled Sophia, the golden flower conceals secrets that require the "cleansing of one's heart," a spiritual purification process, to be revealed.

192

Samadhi	Awakening & absorption into Universal Consciousness
Dhyana	Deep state of meditation
Dharana	One-pointed focus
Pratyahar	Synchronization of senses & thoughts
Pranayam	Control of prana, vital life force
Asana	Postures for health & meditation
Niyama	Five Disciplines
Yama	Five Restraints, behaviors

193   Lu Yan,1668

As translator Richard Wilhelm points out in his opening commentary on *The Secret of the Golden Flower*, the meditations presented in the text aim to "exert a psychic influence on certain processes of the sympathetic nervous system."[194] Evidently, like Jung, Wilhelm had at least a rudimentary understanding of the connection between somatic nervous system processes and the spiritual domain. Just as the parasympathetic feminine portion of the ANS is often suppressed by our Western values of excessive doing, Sophia represents the suppressed feminine power and wisdom of the imaginal realm. Without her, we lack coherence between our intellect and our creative imagination.

The Many Faces of Sophia

Sophia evades those who deprecate her and is elusive to all; to seek her requires disciplined practice. Sophia cannot be pinned down or precisely defined. You may catch the subtle fragrance of her perfume and recognize her as wisdom, beauty, love, and truth. She radiates elevated and universal *cor* values. I use the phrase "lifting the veil" to symbolize the inner transformation required to connect with Sophia.

She is the heart and pulse of evolution, the vibratory matrix of creation (*spanda*) where physical reality is understood as concentrated vibrational energies; she is the dynamic or feminine principle of consciousness. She is Adi Shakti in the form of Saraswati (the Hindu goddess of wisdom) who mobilizes Shiva, absolute consciousness, into spiritual dynamism and vibratory patterns of reality. It is the coherent interaction between the archetypal Shakti and Shiva that makes the physical universe a reality.[195]

Some of Sophia's other names include Inanna, Nüwa, Isis, Mary, Saraswati, Guan Yin, Beatrice, Shakti, Shekinah, Gaea, Brigid, and Erzulie. Every tradition has a name for the feminine aspect of God,

---

194   *The Secret of the Golden Flower*, 1931, p. 4).
195   Kashmir Shaivism identifies Shakti (Sakti) as the power of Shiva (Siva) to create, sustain, and destroy. She is the creative pulsation (Spanda) of Shiva. (Yoga of Vibration and Divine Pulsation, 196).

yet she has been largely veiled from our awareness over the past two millennia. She brings forth creation and yet she lives under the threshold between two worlds, sometimes in the mist or in the light of the moon.

Orthodox theologian Jean-Yves Leloup refers to Sophia as the *nous,* or intermediary, between psyche and spirit, the archetype of synthesis between the masculine and feminine.[196] *Nous* represents the creative imagination that is accessible through the wisdom of the heart rather than the *logos* of the rational mind.

Corbin, writing in *The Heart as a Subtile Organ*, acknowledges that although the connection between the physical and the subtle heart remains essentially unknowable, it is nonetheless within one's potential to experience this connection. In other words, it is possible to begin lifting the veil of Sophia.

The wisdom of Sophia sees through to wholeness and unity. She is not limited to only that which is verifiable. She will not be found in books. She is not to be found in the classroom or in data from laboratory tests. Another word for her might be *gnosis*, wisdom gained from direct experience or intuition that leads to spiritual understanding.

Herman Melville asked, "How many, think ye, have [...] fallen into Plato's honey head, and sweetly perished there?"[197] Humanity is at risk of perishing from an overly inflated masculine ethos. Just as an overactive sympathetic nervous system unbalances the body, an overemphasis on *logos* upsets the masculine-feminine balance (psyche) required for the individuation process, both for the individual and *anima mundi*. But over the past few decades, the pendulum has begun to swing back.

---

196 The Gospel of Mary Magdalene , pp. 103, 119
197 *Moby-Dick* (Melville, 1851)

Unveiling Sophia

In 1895 and 1945, ancient scrolls containing gnostic texts were found in the Upper Egyptian town of Nag Hammadi. These texts are slowly being translated and made available to the public. Elaine Pagels, an American historical scholar and the Harrington Spear Paine Professor of Religion at Princeton University, has been at the forefront of this work. She considers the Gnostic Gospels, as the texts have been named, indispensable for restoring coherence in the Christian tradition and unveiling the feminine heart of Christianity.

Fifty-two early Christian and Gnostic texts, sealed into jars, were inadvertently discovered near a monastery after being buried for almost 2000 years. Scholars suggest that these texts were buried sometime after 367 A.D. in order to protect them from confiscation and certain destruction, as their contents contradicted some of the rulings of the Council of Nicaea under the Bishop of Alexandria, which established the official "New Testament" of Christianity in the mid- fourth century C.E. Any writings that did not agree with the selected texts were deemed heretical.

Initially, the notion that there were other biblical texts struck many—including me—as New Age rhetoric. We had always accepted the Roman Catholic Church's nonnegotiable position that there are only four gospels: Mark, Luke, Matthew, and John. The canon decreed by the Council of Nicaea was deep in our unconscious psyche.

It is not difficult to see, why *The Sophia of Jesus,* one of these texts, was seen as heretical, as it included the assertion that Sophia was Jesus's equal partner. Moreover, the text states that it was She who manifested the Universe:

> The Holy One said to him: "I want you to know that First Man is called 'Begetter, Self-perfected Mind.' He reflected with Great Sophia, his consort, and revealed his first-begotten, androgynous son. His male name is designated 'First Begetter, Son of God,' his female name, 'First Begettress Sophia, Mother of the Universe.' Some call her 'Love.' Now First-begotten is called 'Christ.' Since he has authority from his father, he created a multitude

of angels without number for retinue from Spirit and Light."[198]

Meanwhile, the *Gospel of Mary* taught was that Christ consciousness can be found within every human being: "For it is within you/ That the Son of Man dwells."[199] This powerful concept was hidden from the common people who were taught to worship Christ on the cross, somewhere *out there*, not within themselves.

In the earliest days of Christianity, then, the sacred feminine was considered equal to her masculine counterpart. Another text, the *Pistis Sophia* (Faith in Wisdom), was also hidden to prevent its destruction from the early church fathers under Constantine, the first Christian ruler of Rome. Sophia was reduced to the term "wisdom" devoid of its specifically feminine nature, and the conception of divine feminine power as a true wisdom was expunged from the church— along with the idea that wisdom can be found within and is not held solely in the hands of priests.

Just as the domination of the sympathetic nervous system unbalances the body, the overemphasis on the masculine principle in the church has resulted in a state of dis-ease quite apparent today. In addition to a long practice of killing wise women by decreeing that they were witches, the Church has tolerated predatory priests and covered up their abusive behavior for decades, perpetuating the problem.

Yet as humanity withdraws the projected Christ and meditates on the power within, Christians begin to access the genuine power intended for them. A first step occurred when the Protestant Revolution enabled Bibles to be printed in the vernacular instead of in Latin, allowing any literate person to study the texts for themselves. Later, Sophia's voice began to be heard by luminary Christian

---

198   http://gnosis.org/naghamm/sjc.html "Original translation of this text was prepared by members of the Coptic Gnostic Library Project of the Institute for Antiquity and Christianity, Claremont Graduate School. The Coptic Gnostic Library Project was funded by UNESCO, the National Endowment for the Humanities, and other Institutions."
199   Leloup, 2002, p. 70

thinkers such as the French Jesuit priest Pierre Teilhard de Chardin, who lived from the late 19th to the mid-20th century. "Ever since my childhood I had been engaged in the search for the Heart of Matter, and so it was inevitable that sooner or later I should come up against the Feminine," Teilhard de Chardin declared.[200]

He was also an archeologist who played a key role in the discovery of the Peking Man.[201] His progressive scientific views on evolution soon distanced him from the church,[202] but his notion of the Feminine was also seen as radical. While on the front lines of World War II in France, Teilhard de Chardin wrote his poem on "Eternal Feminine," which includes the lines "I am the magnetic force of the universal presence and ceaseless ripple of its smile./I am the open door to creation"[203] He saw the Eternal Feminine as necessary for unifying our understanding of Christ, through whom "unity is knit together, through which the magnetic power is concentrated."[204] He also wrote about the "Veiled Virgin," the Virgin Mary, and her role in the "total Christ."

The Universal Feminine is an archetype that expresses itself through powerful images that evoke strong emotions. She is on a mission to move life and evolution forward. Sometimes that means destruction of the old and clearing the path before moving forward. The Hindu goddess Kali, with her necklace of skulls and wild eyes and hair, destroys even as she gazes with love on that which she destroys. Death is a part of evolution, and death happens in every moment. As Rumi says, this is "Not the type of death that you go in the grave, [but] /The transforming death, which you go into the light."[205]

---

200 *Heart of Matter*, De Chardin, 1976, p. 58

201 *Homo erectus pekinensis* lived approximately 750,000 years ago.

202 Teilhard wrote: "Evolution is a general condition, to which *all theories, all hypotheses, all systems* must submit and satisfy from now on in order to be conceivable and true" *The Human Phenomenon* (Teilhard de Chardin 1999, 152).

203 Chardin T. d., p. 25.

204 qtd. in De Lubac, 23.

205 Rumi, *Masnawi* Book 6, Part 22

Sophia and Coherence

As the early 19th-century poet John Keats wrote, "Beauty is truth, truth beauty—that is all/Ye know on earth, and all ye need to know." Beauty and truth resonate within psyche, extend beyond the human being, and merge with the matrix of creation. Beauty and truth are that which is in right proportion: the Golden Mean, the Ideal Form. Beauty is not a type of body measured against passing cultural norms (often augmented here and tucked there); beauty follows a higher architecture or pattern of coherence, resonance, and right order. Beauty is an external numinous force operating upon us that evokes an aesthetic response, one drawn from the heart and not the brain. Jung says, "beauty moves *us*, it is not we who create beauty."[206] Beauty can dazzle us, stun us, bewitch us, transfix us.

It is the heart, not the rational brain, that responds to beauty. Beauty is an aspect of love that evokes change. It also optimizes heart coherence: feelings of love cause HRV readings to reach their highest ranges. Love is the great organizer that brings about internal coherence and systemwide order. So, to Keats's words, I would add love. The truth of beauty calls forth love, and this trio is the Divine Feminine, Sophia.

The Eternal Feminine casts her spell through beauty and evokes a reaction. As she effuses the world with beauty, she reaches us through all our senses; the smell of a rose, the sight of Michelangelo's *Pietà*, the sunrise slowly emerging over a mountain range, an exquisite face that draws us on. As Shams-ud-din Muhammad Hafiz, the14th-century Persian mystical poet, wrote in his poem *It Felt Love*:

> How
> Did the rose
> Ever open its heart And give to this world
> All its Beauty?
> It felt the encouragement of light Against its
> Being, Otherwise, We all remain Too Frightened.[207]

---

206   Jung *CW 10* Archaic Man par 139.
207   It Felt Love (Hafiz, 1999).

The mythologist Joseph Campbell and archetypal psychologist James Hillman both talk about the experience of "aesthetic arrest." She does indeed arrest one's soul. Beauty is her siren call, the lure she uses to draw us onto the path to individuation.

The great 14th-century Italian poet Dante Alighieri answered this siren call. His muse was a beautiful young woman, Beatrice, who provoked the writing of Dante's *Divine Comedy*. In this masterpiece, Dante conveys the connection between the incarnated beauty, Beatrice the woman, and the path of individuation with Beatrice as guide in the role of Sophia, the divine Feminine. The ultimate outcome is a mystical union with the divine, the paramount level of coherence. What one truly desires in the end, Dante tells us, is not to possess the beautiful lover; one desires Love itself, "the love that moves the sun and the other stars," as he writes in the last line of the poem. As Plato tells us in Diotima's dialogue with Socrates in the *Symposium*, "love is simply the name for the desire and pursuit of the whole."[208]

Dante knew, as shown in the famous painting,[209] Beatrice as a child, but it was a chance glimpse of her at age 18 that marked him indelibly. Her beauty created a numinous experience, changing him from a heedless youth to a poet. Dante wrote thusly about this encounter: "I say truly that the vital spirit, the one that dwells in the most secret chamber of the heart, began to tremble so violently [. . .] and trembling it spoke these words 'Here is a god stronger than I, who shall come to rule over me'."[210] He was struck trembling and powerless before this mortal embodiment of the Eternal Feminine. From that moment on, his life was "a new life."

The embodied Beatrice died young, and her relationship with Dante was never consummated. Yet her image continued to work deeply on Dante's psyche. In his great poem, Beatrice initiates his pilgrim's journey: "For I am Beatrice who send you on;/ I come from

---

208   193a.

209   Henry Holiday - Dante and Beatrice, https://commons.wikimedia.org/wiki/File:Henry_Holiday_-_Dante_and_Beatrice_-_Google_Art_Project.jpg

210   La Vita Nuova, 1957, p. 3.

where I most long to return;/ Love prompted me, that Love which makes me speak."[211] She understands that Dante has lost his way in the dark woods, a metaphor for the unconscious. Dante has been trapped in a pattern of ego gratification (lusting after women) that leads only to temporary fulfillment, quickly followed by subsequent depletion. Beatrice shows disappointment in Dante's weakness since her death. She calls to him from beyond the grave:

> Nature or art had never showed you any/ beauty that matched the lovely limbs in which
> I was enclosed—limbs scattered now in dust;
> and if the highest beauty failed you through
> my death, what mortal thing could then induce
> you to desire it? For when the first
> arrow of things deceptive struck you, then
> you surely should have lifted up your wings
> to follow me, no longer such a thing[212]

The ego lusts for false beauty, that which is spiritless, carnal, and shallow. Lust involves power over another. One of Dante's self-admitted faults is an egoic desire for power over another, not a balanced dance with the feminine.[213] His task, as with anyone on the path of individuation, is to transmute carnal desire and other expressions of power over another into spiritual love. Love in right proportion (coherence) is the path of transforming lust into love. True love is the joining of spirt and matter so they can resonate together and fuse into one.

Dante recognizes that he needs Beatrice in order to stay the course on his spiritual journey. The divine Feminine is the magnetic force that draws Dante toward his spiritual evolution. His painful confession to Beatrice evinces his awareness:

---

211   Inferno 2 70-72.
212   *Purgatorio* 31. 49-57.
213   The #MeToo movement is a contemporary global refutation of lust that forces itself on another for egoic self- gratification. This perverted form of desire and fulfillment is not in "right order."

Weeping, I answered: 'Mere appearances turned me aside with their false loveliness, as soon as I had lost your countenance'[214]

Full of remorse, he realigns himself with his *cor* values of love, beauty, and spiritual purity. Beatrice as the Divine Feminine is the catalyst for Dante's evolutionary journey, bringing him into coherence with the divine plan and his Hillmanian acorn, his destiny as a poet.

Beatrice as an image of archetypal beauty is the intermediary between Earth and Heaven—the divine drawing a mortal toward itself through the Divine Feminine.

As de Chardin writes, "Love . . . cannot and must not dispense with matter, any more than can the soul . . . so every union of love must begin on the material basis of sensible confrontation and knowledge."[215] Romantic human relationships begin on the physical level, but their destiny is to progress through the continual unveiling of love into spiritual and cosmic expansion. Thus, matter evolves to its spiritual heightened state—a state of coherence with the All.

HRV as a Tool for Unveiling Sophia

Biofeedback techniques have revealed a direct correlation between HRV numbers and states of consciousness. There is a potential association between coherence and consciousness using David R. Hawkins's scale of consciousness;[216] however, rigorous testing is needed to substantiate this possibility. Hawkins used applied kinesiology or biomechanics, the science of muscle testing, to establish states of consciousness. For example, feeling of stress, anger, and anxiety rank below 200 on the Hawkins scale and will likely rank 1 or less on the

---

214   *Purgatorio* 31. 34-36.
215   Chardin T. d., Writings in the Time of War, 1968.
216   David R. Hawkins's map of consciousness uses a scale from 0 to 1000; below 200 represents emotional states from shame to courage (courage being the threshold of higher levels of consciousness). At 250, a state of neutrality appears; from here the scale ascends to willingness, acceptance, reason, love, joy, and peace, finally attaining states of enlightenment at 750-1,000, the highest attainable states of consciousness.

HeartMath® scale (out of 16). If one is experiencing a feeling of joy, the HRV can readily be measured and documented and compared to the Hawkins ranking at 540. Moving beyond emotional states of mind and entering into bliss and the ineffable reflect heightened states of consciousness and approach the upper rungs of both scales. At a broad brush stroke level, there appears to be some correlation between Hawkins's work and coherence scores; however the jury is still out.

Hawkins's theory assumes that Jung is correct and the human psyche has access to a vast pool of information, wisdom, and archetypes held within the collective unconscious. From this infinite wellspring, the individual psyche is able to intuit truth or falsehood. He conjectures that our muscular system responds strongly to the energy fields aligned with truth and goes weak with falsehoods. Hawkins' methodology is outside the boundaries of Western science, at least at the present time.

One can, however, construct a map of one's own consciousness using HRV biofeedback coupled with observation and self-awareness. Most people can self-identify the emotional states mentioned above and could then associate the emotion with HRV biofeedback results. By correlating one's state of being with HRV results, one can construct one's own map of consciousness over the course of several weeks or months.

My personal experience has been that HRV coherence scores over 10 (using a scoring system of 0 to 16) correlate with a deep state of meditation much like a trance state. My hypothesis is that states that are often described with terms like enlightenment, *samadhi*, or bliss approach 16 on the scale. Advanced meditative states, including *Samadhi*, *Shuniya*, Christ consciousness, or Pure Bliss, theoretically begin at 700 and above on the Hawkins scale and approach 16 on the HM scale.[217] Here is where the light of consciousness is unveiled. The challenge is to quiet one's mind through meditation, prayer, or

---

217   Please note that this assertion is the conjecture of the author, and not intended to represent the perspective of the HeartMath® Institute.

mindfulness to allow higher states of awareness to break through. The unitive state of oneness is ever present and emerges once the veil is removed.

And as this book has made plain, oneness requires union with the feminine. We must learn to incorporate feminine principles or we will die physically or psychically, both as individuals and as a society. As the ANS awakens, the parasympathetic for heart health we also transform and increase our ability for compassion.

Increasing compassion can be learned, even in adulthood, through the stimulation of the vagus nerve. When the parasympathetic nervous system is activated, the fight/flight/freeze state subsides, allowing one to care for others and positive social behavior to flourish. A cycle of compassionate behavior invokes positive results for others, which benefits both giver and receiver. People can train themselves to stimulate the vagus nerve through biofeedback using HRV as a measure of how well they are doing.

Researchers from The Center for Compassion and Altruism Research and Education at Stanford University argue that "the field of compassion science needs to move toward including HRV as a primary outcome measure in its future assessment and training, due to its connection to vagal regulatory activity, and its link to overall health and well-being."[218, 219] Compassion is a feminine quality, and when it is restored, not just the heart, but ancient wounds get healed.

---

218   Kirby J. N., 2017, "The Current and Future Role of Heart Rate Variability for Assessing and Training Compassion".

219   Also see Lehrer, Paul M., and Richard Gevirtz. "Heart Rate Variability Biofeedback: How and Why Does It Work?" *Frontiers in Psychology* 5 (2014): 756. *PMC*. Web. 11 Sept. 2018.

Lectio Divina: The Ancient Practice of Sacred Reading

I stumbled upon the act of Lectio Divina (Latin for Divine Reading), as many incredible things in life, by accident. Although typically associated with the Christian practice of reading and meditating on Scripture, I have found the essence of Psalm 46, "Be still and know that I am God," for myself after reading a wide array of sacred and secular literature. For the purpose of this experiential exercise, I define Lectio Divina as any reading that opens the "eye of the heart."

As part of my own individuation process, I read inspiring works most mornings before the business of the day sets in. At times, I practice heart coherence biofeedback training directly after reading. I noticed that some reading sessions appear to precipitate unusually high coherence scores compared with my average baseline. I hypothesize that readings that generate high heart coherence are ones that I resonate strongly with, quite literally. There is a core element of truth that my psyche-soma is picking up as true, beautiful, or other high-frequency emotion.

Originally, it was slightly startling to see (through biofeedback) the physiological impact that reading certain books and articles was having on me. Again, obtaining high heart coherence is not a one-size-fits-all approach. Get curious and discover what effect reading has on your psyche-soma. Many people instinctively can tell you which books get them into the "flow" or "zone," yet many of us have become disconnected from our heart centers.

The sequence of practicing Lectio Divina is as follows:

- ♥ **Read:** meditative reading of sacred text
- ♥ **Meditate:** *meditatio*, reflecting upon the meaning of the sacred text
- ♥ **Pray:** *oratio*, communication with God
- ♥ **Contemplate:** *contemplatio*, quiet resting in God

I have modified the traditional sequence of Lectio Divina and combine the meditative and prayer aspects, which I view as having significant overlap. Essentially, I read, meditate (optionally using biofeedback), then listen to the intuition and wisdom of my heart. When the heart enters a state of high coherence, it is possible to tap into its wisdom with little interference from the static of the mind.

Coherence and resonance are an alignment to a higher truth, not of the ego, but of the Self.

EXPERIENTIAL PRACTICE

Use the excerpt below or select one of your own choosing.

Read: meditative reading of sacred texts, including making notations.

Meditate: becoming silent and still without the active use of the mind.

Listen for heart wisdom or intuition, "listen to God's [or Universe, Creative Potential, or your preferred term] word with the ear of the heart" as Saint Benedict instructed.

Allow yourself to drift into a meditative state where you lean into the imaginal edge of the unconscious. Make note of images that especially sparked your imagination.

The following excerpt was authored by Ibn 'Arabi, who, as part of the Sufi tradition, recognized Sophia as the Divine Feminine intermediary between human souls and Divine (qtd. Creative Imagination in Sufism, p 175 or Llewellyn Vaughan-Lee, The Return of the Feminine, 189).

Dearly Beloved!
I have called you so often and you have not heard me.
I have shown myself to you so often and you have not seen me.
I have made myself fragrance so often, and you have not /smelled me, Savorous food, and you have not tasted me.

Why can you not reach me through the object you touch
Or breathe me through sweet perfumes?
Why do you not see me? Why do you not hear me?
Why? Why? Why?

> For you my delights surpass all other delights,
> And the pleasure I procure you surpasses all other /pleasures.
> For you I am preferable to all other good things,
> I am Beauty, I am Grace.

Love me, love me alone.
Love yourself in me, in me alone.
Attach yourself to me,
No one is more inward than I.
Others love you for their own sakes, I love you for yourself.
And you, you flee from me.

> Dearly beloved!
> You cannot treat me fairly,
> For if you approach me,
> It is because I have approached you.

I am nearer to you than yourself,
Than your soul, than your breath.
Who among creatures
Would treat you as I do?
I am jealous of you over you,
I want you to belong to no other,
Not even to yourself.
Be mine, be for me as you are in me,
Though you are not even aware of it.

Dearly beloved!
Let us go toward Union.
And if we find the road
That leads to separation,
We will destroy separation.

Let us go hand in hand.
Let us enter the presence of Truth.
Let it be our judge
And imprint its seal upon our union
For ever.

Creative Imagination in the Sufism of Ibn Arabi, p 174-175

When you are finished with the above three steps, take several minutes or more writing in your journal. Engage in a conversation (active imagination) with Sophia, the one who speaks in the poem.

Conclusion

"When the patient found the yellow piece of amber and it began to beat like a heart, and the earth and trees and all of nature joined in the rhythm, [. . .] it was a moment of Tao"

—C. G. Jung (*Visions 2* 676)

While new battles are being won daily on the technology front, the war is being lost in areas such as chronic diseases, addictions, and the environmental crisis. Politicians argue about the health care crisis, but do not address its taproot—the collective impact of chronic stress.

Stress accounts for upwards of 90% of all doctor visits, and either the doctor medicates us, or we do it ourselves with alcohol, consumerism, opioids, etc. When problems are pushed underground new ones crop up in other areas. Our antidotes to stress take us further down the path of addictions, loss of meaning, and chronic diseases.

As we continue to limit our vision to *logos* to solve global problems, our collective crises intensify. Chronic stress creates chaotic heart rhythm patterns in individuals, the theme of Chapter Three, the disharmony spreads outwards evidenced by chronic diseases, opioid addictions, and suicides.

More effective solutions will arise as we collectively utilize the full spectrum of human intelligence, *logos* and Sophia. As with the rainmaker in Chapter Five, as we each take responsibility to get ourselves, families, and communities into "right order" (coherence) we sync us with the larger system wide order. The hinge pin in all of this is the heart, and its inherent feminine wisdom.

WORKS CITED

Aird, W. C. (2011). Discovery of the cardiovasuclar system: from Galen to William Harvey . *J Thromb Haemost* , 118-129.

al, S. F. (2017). An Overview of Heart Rate Variability Metrics and Norms. *Front. PublicHealth, 5*(258).

Alighieri, D. (1957). *La Vita Nuova.* (M. Musa, Trans.) New Brunswick, NJ: Rutgers UniversityPress.

Bohm, D. (1996). *On Creativity.* New York, NY: Routledge Classics.

Buckberg, G. D. (2002, November). Basic science review: The helix and the heart. *The Journalof Thoracic and Cardiovascular Surgery*, 863-883.

Buckberg MD, G. D. (2002, November). Basic Science Review: The Helix and the Heart. *TheJournal of Thoracic and Cardiovascular Surgery*, 863-883.

Chardin, P. T. (1976). *The Heart of Matter.* New York, NY: Harcourt.

Chardin, T. d. (n.d.). The Eternal Feminine. In T. d. Chardin, *Writings in Time of War* (R. Hague,Trans.). New York, NY: Harper and Row.

Cook, D. J. (1981). "The Pre-Established Harmony between Leibniz and Chinese Thought."

Journal of the History of Ideas, 42(2), 253-267.

Corbin, H. (1994). *The Man of Light: in Iranian Sufism* (arrangement by Shambala ed.). (N.Pearson, Trans.) New Lebanon, NY: Omega Publications Inc.

Cowan MD, T. (2016). Human Heart, Cosmic Heart: A Doctor's Quest to Understand, Treat, andPrevent Cardiovascular Disease. White River Junction, VT: Chelsea Green Publishing.

De Chardin, P. T. (1976). *The Heart of Matter.* New York, NY: Harvest Book/ Harcourt, Inc. Descartes, R. (1999). *Discourse on Method and Meditations on First Philosophy* (4th ed.). (D. A.Cress, Trans.) Indianapolis, IN: Hackett Publishing Company.

Edinger, E. F. (1995). *The Mysterium Lectures: A journey through C. G. Jung's MysteriumConiunctionis.* (J. D. Blackmer, Ed.) Toronto, Canada: Inner City Books.

Gerald Buckberg, M. (2015, September 29). The Helical Heart .

Goethe, J. W. (2006). *The Green Snake and the Beautiful Lily.* (J. d. Allen, Ed., & J. E. Heuscher, Trans.) Great Barrington, MA: Steiner Books.

Goethe, J. W. (n.d.). *Faust: Part 2.* (D. Constantine, Trans.) New York, NY: Penguin Classics.Goethe, J. W. (n.d.). *Goethe's Theory of Colours.* (C. L. Eastlake, Trans.)

Govinda, L. A. (n.d.). *The Inner Structure of the I Ching: The Book of Transformations.* SanFrancisco, CA: Wheelhouse Press.

Gray, J. F. (1987). *The History of Mathematics: A Reader 1987th Edition*. (J. F. Gray, Ed.)London, UK: Macmillan Education.

Harvey, W. (n.d.). *De Motu Cordis: Movement of the Heart and Blood in Animals* . (K. J.Franklin, Trans.) Blackwell Scientific Publications Badgers Books.

Hawkins, D. R. (2002). *Power vs. Force: the Hidden Determinants of Human Behavior.*Carlsbad, CA: Hay House.

HeartMath®. (n.d.). *HeartMath.org/articles*. Retrieved June 15, 2018, from https://www.heartmath.org/articles-of-the-heart/the-math-of-heartmath/heart-intelligence/ HeartMath. (n.d.). Science of the Heart: Exploring the Role of the Heart in Human PerformanceAn Overview of Research Conducted by the HeartMath® Institute.

Hillman, J. (1997). *A Blue Fire*. (T. Moore, Ed.) New York, NY: Harper Perennial.

Hillman, James. *Alchemical Psychology (Uniform Edition of the Writings of James Hillman Book 5)*. Spring Publications. Thompson, CT, 2015

Hillman, J. (2004). *The Thought of the Heart and the Soul of the World*. Putnam, CT: SpringPublications, Inc.

Ho, M.-W. (2002). *The Rainbow and the Worm: The Physics of Organisms* (2nd ed.). Singapore:World Scientific Publishing.

Jung, C. G. (1970). *Alchemical Studies The Collected Works of C. G. Jung. Vol. 13* (Vol. 13). (R.

F. Hull, Trans.) Princeton, NJ: Princeton UP.

Jung, C. G. (1989). *Mysterium Coniunctionis* (Vol. 14). Princeton, NJ: Princeton UniversityPress.

Jung, C. G. (1996). The Psychology of Kundalini Yoga: Notes of the Seminar Given in 1932 by

C.G. Jung. (S. Shamdasani, Ed.) Princeton, NJ: Princeton UP.

Jung, C. G. (1997). *Visions: Notes of the Seminar Given in 1930-1943* (Vol. 2). (C. Douglas,Ed.) Princeton, NJ: Princeton University Press.

Jung, C. G. (n.d.). *Collected Works 8*.

Jung, C. G. (n.d.). *Memories, Dreams, Reflections*. (A. Jaffé, Ed., & R. A. Winston, Trans.) NewYork, NY: Random House, Inc.

Jung, C. G. (n.d.). The Collected Works of C.G. Jung: Complete Digital Edition (Vols. 1-19). Jung, C. G., & Henderson, J. (2002). *The Earth Has a Soul: C.G. Jung on Nature, Technology &Modern Life*. (M. Sabini, Ed.) Berkeley, CA: North Atlantic Books.

Kirby, J. N. (2017, September). "The Current and Future Role of Heart Rate Variability forAssessing and Training Compassion." *Frontiers in Public Health* .

Leloup, J.-Y. (2002). *The Gospel of Mary Magdaene* . (J.-Y. Leloup, Trans.) Rochester, VT:Inner Traditions.

London, S. (2012, July 01). On Soul, Character and Calling: A Conversation with JamesHillman. (J. Hillman, Interviewer)

McCraty, R. (n.d.). *The Energetic Heart.*

Muller-Orte. (n.d.).

Muller-Ortega, P. E. (1989). The Triadic Heart of Siva: Kaula Tantricism of Abhinavagupta inthe Non-Dual Shaivism of Kashmir. Albany, NY: SUNY Press.

Narby, J. (1998). *The Cosmic Serpent: DNA and the Origins of Knowledge.* New York, NY:Jeremy P Tarcher/Putnam.

Needham, J. W. (1956). *Science and Civilisaton in China, History of Scientific Thought* (Vol. 2).New York, NY: Cambridge University Press.

Ober, C. S. (2014). *Earthing: The Most Important Health Discovery Ever!* Columbus, OH: BasicHealth Publications, Inc. .

O'Regan, C. E. (2014). "Antidepressants strongly influence the relationship between depressionand heart rate variability: findings from The Irish Longitudinal Study on Ageing (TILDA)".

Psychological medicine, vol. 45,3, 623-36.

Parker, A. (Director). (1996). *Evita* [Motion Picture].

Powers, D. (n.d.). *William Harvey.* London, England: T. Fisher Unwin.

Ridker, P. M. (2017, August 27). Inflammation reduction cuts risk of heart attack, stroke. (H. B.Communications, Interviewer) *The Harvard Gazette.*

Sannella, L., MD. *The Kundalini Experience: Psychosis or Transcendence.* Lower Lake, CA. H. S. Dakin Company, 1987.

Sardello, R. J. (2004). *Facing the World with Soul: The Reimagination of Modern Life.* GreatBarrington: Lindisfarne Books.

Stanford University. (n.d.). *A History of the Heart.* Retrieved 06 14, 2018, from web. stanford.edu: https://web.stanford.edu/class/history13/earlysciencelab/body/ heartpages/heart.html

Steiner, R. (2003). *Isis Mary Sophia: Her Mission and Ours.* (C. Bamford, Ed.) GreatBarrington, MA: Steiner Books.

Strogatz, S. (2003). *Sync: How Order Emerges from Chaos in the Universe, Nature, and DailyLife.* New York, NY: Hachette Books.

Swiderski, R. M. (1980). Bouvet and Leibniz: A Scholarly Correspondence. *Eighteenth-CenturyStudies, 14*, 135-150.

Taylor, A. E. (2008, March 30). Evita! What Kind of Goddess has Lived Among Us?

Unpublished Essay. Camano Island: Unpublished Essay.

Vaughan-Lee, L. (2017). *The Return of the Feminine and the World Soul.* Point Reyes, CA: TheGolden Sufi Center.

Wilhelm, R. (1997). *The* I Ching *or Book of Changes* (Vol. Bollingen Series XIX). (R. Wilhelm,Trans.) Princeton University Press.

World Spirituality. (1987). *Islamic Spirituality Foundations* (Vol. 19). (S. H. Nasr, Ed.) NewYork, NY: Crossroad Publishing Company.

Wright, T. (2013). *William Harvey: A Life in Circulation*. New York, NY: Oxford UniversityPress.

Yogi Bhajan, P. G. (1998). *The Mind: Its Projections and Multiple Facets*. Santa Cruz, CA:Kundalini Research Institute.

APPENDIX A: CASE STUDIES

Roland's Post-Heart Surgery Experience

> *"A man's work is nothing but this slow trek to rediscover, through the detours of art, those two or three great and simple images in whose presence his heart first opened."*
>
> — Albert Camus, Youthful Writings

Roland's case study is presented here as an experiential practice because his story provides an example of how archetypal symbols can have a profound impact on our lives. My first introduction to Roland[220] was at a *Kundalini* yoga workshop in Seattle focusing on the heart and opening the heart *chakra*. Roland, the workshop teacher, briefly shared his personal story of how his life changed after quadruple bypass heart surgery. The life-altering event had significant ramifications to his lifestyle and provided the recognition that he had become estranged from his *cor* values. His inner voice had long been silenced but now asserted itself.

Roland grew up in the 1950s and '60s on the East Coast in the United States, and common for men of his generation, the cultural norm was to suppress emotions. The mantra that boys don't cry was an unfortunate mandate of that era and still exists to a degree today.

Exceptionally bright, Roland graduated from MIT and Harvard in engineering and started a family following the yellow brick road of the American dream. Getting an Ivy League education essentially guaranteed his financial success, but one must stay within the bounds of the "road" of accepted cultural norms. His energies were focused

---

220   The name has been changed to respect his privacy.

on work and raising his family, and he remained unaware of his lack of emotional connectedness to his life. Emotions go underground or into the unconscious psyche when split off, but they do not go away.

As his stress levels increased, so did his drinking pattern, as is a common response to unmanaged stress. The ritual of the three-martini night numbed whatever discontent was trying to ring through. Alcohol consumption (and other addictive patterns) is a common antidote to stress, albeit a very dangerous one because emotions get suppressed, and eventually the blocks give way in unpredictable ways. After 25 years of stressful work and a life of "going through the motions," a stress test revealed that four of his coronary arteries were 90 percent blocked.

Without delay, Roland went into surgery for a quadruple bypass before he had time to process what was happening. As he was returning to consciousness in the recovery room, an image spontaneously emerged before him. His heart released a Hillmanian "spark of consciousness" in the form of an image, the symbolic language of psyche. The wisdom held within his wounded body incurred by major heart surgery was released. The mythopoetic lyrics of Leonard Cohen's *Anthum* express it thusly: "There is a crack in everything/ That's how the light gets in." Through the "crack" in one's daily life, consciousness has the potential to break through. As the ego becomes more vulnerable, there is a tendency for it to surrender, because it realizes that it does not have total control of life-altering events.

A life-threatening cardiac event forces awareness away from one's routine egoic processes as the injured organ takes center stage, as in Roland's case. You are dealing with the shock that you are critically ill and the pathway to recovery is typically outside one's own egoic control. A person cannot *will* health, which may be experienced as a defeat for the ego or a loss of control over one's fate. This shift of ego consciousness serves as a threshold for the individuation process—a letting-go of false constructs of the egoic self in favor of the higher authority of the Self. In the Jungian sense of the word, Self is the central organizing principle of the psyche that transcends the conscious awareness and represents the archetype of wholeness.

From a depth psychology viewpoint, the term Self does not necessarily imply a core of divine essence; rather, Jung viewed Self as "the principle and archetype of orientation and meaning." (*MDR* 199) The line between divine core, Self in the Eastern sense, and Jung's notion of Self became blurred when he succinctly posed the question: "Is he [or she] related to something infinite or not?" (*MDR* 325) That which is infinite transcends a rational definition; therefore, it is nearly impossible to determine the overlap between the traditional notion of divine Self and the Jungian notion of Self, which contains a numinous core.

Returning now to Roland's postsurgical experience, upon awakening from the anesthesia, a symbol appeared to him in the form of letter "C," which he experienced as being imprinted onto his heart. Without intellectualizing the symbol, he immediately intuited what his heart was communicating, and told me that "it rang to my core." For Roland, the "C" symbolized compassion. Compassion for himself was the first order of business. He was not living the truth of who he was, and although involved with spiritual work beforehand, he recognized that his approach had been an intellectual exercise. His heart was calling him to bring forth compassion, for himself and others.

Roland was receptive to the "message" and was grateful for it. His heretofore out-of-balance masculine approach to life was now making room for his feminine *cor* values, beginning with compassion. Roland shared that his life-threatening experience did not leave him with a feeling of being a "victim" of heart disease; rather, he viewed the disease as delivering an urgent message of needed change. With this insight, he revamped his life; first, he left his relationship, which he viewed as existing without emotion. In time, his career shifted into more compatible work with his new way of being in the world, a fully human being holding both the masculine and feminine attributes of himself.

Sitting across from Roland as our time together was ending, I witnessed a vibrant man who was genuinely filled with love for life and passion for helping other people through his coaching and yoga practices. By integrating his *cor* value of compassion into his work, life, and relationships, he rebalanced the masculine (*logos*/thinking) with the feminine trait of compassion (feeling with empathy). He was indeed living his insights, walking his talk, and his life was brimming with meaning, and that is not to be confused with a lack of challenges. Living your authentic life takes courage.

What is most meaningful to you, your *cor* values, is not what someone else wants for you or tried to mold you into regardless of how well intended it appears on the surface; rather, your *cor* values are imprinted upon your heart, and essentially it is one's challenge to discover them. Although an acute illness temporarily opens a portal that is not otherwise readily accessible, it remains the responsibility of the individual to discover his/her *cor* values. Surprisingly, many people do not know, for they were silenced many years ago.

For Roland, two of his key *cor* values that he previously wasn't living are compassion and truth. By taking responsibility for his condition, making constructive changes, and not allowing fear and despair to overwhelm him, he was able to experience a fuller spectrum of life and no longer lived on autopilot devoid of emotion.

Everyone's experience with a life-threatening illness is unique. As the high incidence of postcardiac-event depression[221] suggests, the ego mind often feels defeated by the trauma of a cardiac event.

Questions for Reflection

♥ Can you recall any dream symbols that emerged at critical junctures in your life?

♥ In what ways did the symbols or dream image inform your life going forward, if at all?

♥ Have you experienced any recurring dreams over the years? Can you reflect back and find a deeper connection with your life?

---

221 *The Harvard Heart Letter* reported: "Recovering from a heart attack is tough enough without facing depression. Yet that's exactly what happens to nearly half of heart attack survivors." https://www.health.harvard.edu/press_releases/depression-and-heart-disease. Also see: Dhar, A. K., & Barton, D. A. (2016). Depression and the Link with Cardiovascular Disease. *Frontiers in psychiatry, 7,* 33. doi:10.3389/fpsyt.2016.00033

Lillian and the Emergence of the Divine Feminine

This chapter is a case study showcasing a woman's encounter with embodied *kundalini* energy and the emergence of the Divine Feminine, personally and in a cosmic sense. I came to know Lillian (not her real name) as a participant in a workshop series that I led in the winter of 2017, titled *The Heroine's Journey to a Coherent Heart*. The workshop focused on the basic concepts presented in Section I, augmented with a daily *Kundalini* meditation.[222] Lillian contacted me before the workshop and shared the following dream, which led her to the workshop. All three aspects of the hearts discussed throughout this book (coherent, archetypal, cosmic heart of Sophia) become relevant during Lillian's process.

Lillian's Call to Adventure: Expand the Light Within Your Heart

"I am talking very intently to a man. He is a Jewish man with dark hair and a beard. I tell this man, very insistently, that the reason we are here, in this life on Earth, is to enlarge our hearts. That is why we are here and that is our purpose or mission for being alive. I am talking very intently and insistently to him. I hold up my thumb and pointer finger to make a small circle gesture. I say something like, 'This is the (size of the) light in our hearts, and we must make it bigger.'"

In the depth psychological lexicon, Lillian's dream would be characterized as a "big dream," one which has the potential to alter the trajectory of one's life. Lillian had been called to "make the light bigger" within her heart . . . and beyond. The archetypal language of dream images often requires deciphering, and subsequent images and sensory experiences were to follow Lillian's dream to make the task more complex in some ways yet unifying in essential ways.

---

222   *Kundalini* Yoga as taught by Yogi Bhajan. Anne Elizabeth Taylor is a KRI certified *Kundalini* Yoga instructor and licensed HeartMath® provider.

Unlike Roland's single vision image discussed earlier, Lillian received a progressive series of dream images rich in alchemical and number symbolism. Months after the aforementioned dream, she had sensory experiences consistent with descriptions of awakening *kundalini* energy to add to the psychic mix. Such symptoms may include, but not limited to:

♥ Sensations of energy ascending through the body (mild to severe)

♥ Heat

♥ Lights and sounds

♥ Vision patterns

♥ Pain

♥ Spontaneous movements, including yoga positions

♥ Unusual breathing patterns

The above symptoms are further discussed in *The Kundalini Experience: Psychosis or Transcendence* by Lee Sannella, MD[223].

To begin, Lillian's own association with the Jewish man (she herself is not Jewish) is unclear; however, she associated the image with the terms "patriarchy" and "wisdom, perhaps the male version of wisdom." From a Jungian perspective, Lillian was likely dialoguing with her *animus* (Latin for spirit), the portion of her psyche guided by *logos,* or the masculine principle. Growing the light of the heart is a call to rebalance the internal dynamics between *logos* and her feminine intuitive wisdom, *Sophia.*

The phrase "growing the light of the heart" used in this book corresponds to increasing heart coherence, first, somatically, which ripples into psychological and spiritual coherence. As heart coherence increases, the reflective nature of the heart expands by "polishing the mirror of the heart" in terms of the Sufi tradition or other contemplative practices. Sufis believe that the heart is a unique vehicle capable

---

223   Lee Sannella, MD. *The Kundalini Experience: Psychosis or Transcendence.* Lower Lake, CA. H. S. Dakin Company, 1987.

of reflecting both the human and divine. As one gazes into the heart mirror, it is believed that one can indirectly see the divine reflected back. The heart serves as the gateway by which the divine sees us, and we see It, but only if the heart is clear of impurities or "dust." Similarly, Ancient Egyptian mythology describes the "weighing of the heart" by the god Anubis after death to ensure its lightness achieved through a life of good deeds and conduct in accord with the law. The heart was weighted against the "Feather of Ma'at," Egyptian goddess and principle of truth, authenticity, balance, order, harmony, among other attributes symbolizing coherence. The heart had to be at least as light as Ma'at's feather in order for the dead person to pass through to the afterlife, otherwise s/he was devoured by the goddess Ammat. The concept of the heart and right order, coherence, runs through the world mythologies, and it does today, as in Lillian's case.

Lillian's journey involves the discovery of what the seemingly cryptic message "increasing the light of the heart" is specifically asking of her. How does one go about "polishing the mirror" of the heart? The Sufis and many Wisdom traditions teach that prayer is the secret to keeping the heart mirror clean. In depth psychological terms, active imagination[224] is another avenue to cleaning the heart mirror and allowing its intrinsic light to shine brighter. To move further into the dream image, active imagination between the dreamer and the dream figure could yield deeper insights of personal significance. As previously discussed, we are free to accept or refuse the call or challenge. Many people brush off dreams as just that, being "only" a dream.

However, dream images can linger for years, resurfacing again and again, until psyche's message reaches the conscious mind.

Big dreams such as this one startle the ego, the part of oneself that is content with the status quo, especially when *it* is in charge. A dream nudges one out of day-to-day complacency and often threatens the ego's position of power. This is the journey we are all called to embark

---

224   Active imagination, or trancing, is a Jungian technique of dialoging with symbolic images from the unconscious to bridge the conscious and unconscious psyche and bring forth salient information.

on: to shift one's power base from ego to Self. To refuse the call is to refuse life. The terms "hero" and "heroine" imply courage, the bravery needed to face the certain dangers (initiation phase) that will inevitably arise. Everyone has his or her own unique journey to undertake and to do the hard work of self-exploration, which requires descending into the unconscious.

Dreamwork is a portal to the unconscious realm filled with uncertainties. In his elder years, Jung remarked, "Anyone who takes the sure road is as good as dead." *(Memories, Dreams, Reflections*, p. 297) In other words, to stay with the ego's agenda is to live a life based on superficial or material desires rather than developing the callings of psyche, the soul, and Sophia. This brings back the notion of living in accord with one's *cor* values, innate values emanating from one's heart center. To do so requires tremendous courage, which is the threshold of higher heart coherence[225].

While the portal to your inner being will likely look different from someone else's, the shared purpose is to transform your inner "lead into gold," alchemically speaking. Such an alchemical transformation requires a shift of internal power, from one based on the ego's wants and fears to the powerhouse of the Self, whose language is archetypal images. The "decoding" of such images comes through intuitive heart wisdom, Sophia (not the rational mind). Sophia of the heart intuits archetypal messages and their meaning to Self and *anima mundi*, the soul of the world.

Returning now to Lillian's participation in the workshop, the "Meditation to Heal a Broken Heart"[226] was the first designated meditation because of its relative simplicity and suitability for beginners. Although simple to practice, this meditation can have powerful effects on the ANS and the subtle pressure it puts on the heart meridian. It is one way of "polishing the mirror of the heart." The *mudra*, hand position, places the palms together in prayer pose and aligns the tips

---

225   Hawkins scale of consciousness ranks courage at the level of 200, the threshold point where one pulls oneself out of negative states of being.
226   Meditation to Heal a Broken Heart, originally taught by Yogi Bhajan March 26, 1975.

of the middle fingers with the third eye point (between the eyebrows). Whether one's heart is "broken" due to a disconnect from one's own Self or in relationship to another through death, divorce, addictions or numerous other possibilities, the nervous system and brain may be affected by emotional and physical separation. This ancient meditation is designed to rebalance the nervous system and quell emotional storms. Some practitioners, however, may be primed for a *kundalini* experience, and even a seemingly simple practice can tip the scale, so to speak, and bring the experience forward. This assumes that the practitioner was at the brink of the experience and it would have likely occurred regardless. Afterward, I had the sense that Lillian intuited this process was immanent and sought out resources to help her "birth" her *kundalini* as the following sequences suggest.

Lillian brought to my attention a rather unusual physical occurrence she experienced as she practiced this meditation. In her own words, she reported the following (2-14-2018): *"As I was doing [the] 11-minute meditation,*[227] *I felt a shiver come from below and run up my spine. This made me think of the phrase 'kundalini rising.' It also reminded me of a powerful snake dream that I had last year in which a snake came to me face to face and struck me. I awoke from that dream with a violent start as I was being struck by the snake!"*

Unlike more dramatic recounts of *kundalini* awakening experiences, such as the one reported by Gopi Krishna in *Kundalini: The Evolutionary Energy of [Hu]man* (Krishna, 1967), Lillian's experience was relatively mild and not debilitating. Her nervous system may have been more prepared to receive the "higher spiritual wattage" of emerging *kundalini* energy, which is my speculation as to what was happening to her during the episodes of "shivers" rising up her spine. Although not well documented at this point in time, there appears to be a wide variation in people's experience of awakening *kundalini*. *Kundalini* research is a new frontier in the Western paradigm. Dream images that proceeded the physical symptoms of Lillian's awakening *kundalini* substantiated my theory (and will be discussed shortly). Before

---

227   I use the term "11 Minute Meds" to convey the medical grade potential of *Kundalini* yogic meditations when performed for 11 minutes.

considering her dream series, a follow-up report from Lillian about her physical symptoms as they are related to her dream symbolism:

> 2-16-2018 "Today I practiced the 'Meditation to Heal a Broken Heart' for the third consecutive day. I felt active energy in me and I was beset by two strong shivers up my torso. I am left with a feeling of active energy coursing around my body. And I also have a visual disturbance [lasting approximately 30 minutes, which she had previously experienced as well]. When I look out from my eyes it looks as if I am looking through a clear kaleidoscope. There are shimmering shapes in my vision."

Upon this reported experience, I reduced the frequency and duration of her meditation, which quelled the symptoms. Since I am not a medical doctor, I did not want to inadvertently precipitate any underlying illness that might have been present. It is important to note that Lillian did not display any symptoms that were detectable by traditional Western doctors, and there didn't appear to be anything clinically discernable. It is possible for *kundalini*-like symptoms to overlap with or be completely attributable to psychosis; conversely, psychosis may be misdiagnosed when the person is actually undergoing *kundalini* activation.

> 2-18-2018 "I just want to report back that I did the gentle meditation for 3 minutes this morning and felt 'bright' but not over energized afterwards."

Lillian further shared that she was unfamiliar with "*kundalini*" (aside from the phrase "*kundalini* rising"), however, she gestured the shimmying serpentine movement going up her spine. The primordial sine wave motion of the serpent is held deep within psyche, and whether a person is aware of "*kundalini*" or not, this psychic energy is common to all of humanity.

It may be possible that her sensory disturbances were related to pineal gland secretions often associated with *kundalini* activation; however, this speculation moves beyond the intended scope of this book. The "kaleidoscope" visions that Lillian experienced are possibly linked with sensory transformation, a hallmark of *kundalini* awakening. The kaleidoscope vision could also be a neurological repercussion of psychic dismantling prior to rebuilding and rebirthing the Self.

It is important to note that Lillian did not display any symptoms that were detectable by traditional Western doctors, and there didn't appear to be anything clinically discernable. Lillian did not seem particularly alarmed by her experiences; however, she clearly wanted to better understand what was happening to her. After the workshop concluded, Lillian contacted me to better understand her autumn of 2016 dream series.

Lillian's Dream Visions (Autumn of 2016)

What was most helpful to the process of working with Lillian and her dream series was her intuitive paintings, which she completed shortly after the dream images emerged. Dream images have a tendency to evaporate or morph into forms once the intellect becomes involved. By using art as a medium, she was able to let go of rational thinking about the images and let her creative imagination flow. Without conscious awareness, she included important subtleties such as color, emotional tone, and numbers. Such nuances, particularly when viewed in a dream series, provides a rich layer of meaning otherwise easily overlooked. All the points on the road through the individuation process, the hero's or heroine's journey, are reflections or parts of the whole process. Each "separate" dream image in Lillian's series links with and to the others to form a continuum where each image helps to inform the others.

One benefit of actively engaging with dream images through art (and other forms) is that the unconscious psyche provides indicators not obvious to the conscious mind, as we will see shortly. Rather than initially focusing on the "meaning" of the dream symbols, painting allows the images to be guided by intuition, the internal feminine mode of knowing, and captured as *prima materia* to work with at some point in the future. Dream images are the symbolic language of psyche with unfathomable depths, and to prematurely assign "meaning" stunts the process.

Jung expressed the importance of capturing nuanced images thusly:

> "I took great care to understand every single image, every item of my psychic inventory, and to classify them scientifically—so far as this was possible—and, above all, to realize them in actual life. That is what we usually neglect to do. We allow the images to rise up, and maybe we wonder about them, but that is all" (*Memories, Dreams, Reflections* 192).

It is not sufficient to "look up" an image in a dream dictionary and say, "There, I have it, I have interpreted the dream!" To do so is to kill the archetypal image, which has the potential to evoke deeper meanings over time. A dream image will continue to unfold as the symbol expresses itself in magnificent ways. Such was the case for Lillian, whose earlier dream images continue to unfold as she progresses along on her spiritual path of individuation. Without knowledge of *kundalini* or Jungian psychology, her active engagement with psychic material allowed the images to speak to her without egoic filtration, that is to say, where the logical mind, *logos*, wants answers. Her paintings emerged from her intuitive heart, not her logical head.

Images of Transformation:
The Feminine Side of Individuation

Painting is one way to give "form" to unconscious content and exemplifies Jung's process of active imagination. Also called "trancing," active imagination allows the dreamer, or visioner, to consciously (or more appropriately, semiconsciously) engage with unconscious contents that appear in symbol language.

Goethe's poem segment is a Jungian invocation (intended or not) into trancing, or active imagination. Goethe surrenders into a passionate plea with Hāfiz ((1315-90)) as he is brought to ecstatic longing:

Goethe to Hāfiz[228]:

Let the world perish, Hāfiz, so
I vie with you, only with you!
Let us be twin-born brothers, two
That share our joy and share our woe!
To love and drink as you would do:
This is my pride and my life too
("Unbounded" Goethe's *West-Östlicher Diwan* 63).

This vivid communication "imagines" the intimate relationship forward, not in a sexual sense; rather, in the Sufic sense between lover and Beloved. Goethe soars beyond the realm of time and space; his passion and love for Hāfiz are in the liminal moment of the imagination. His is not an intellectual exercise; it is heart-centered experience in the realm of the *mundus imaginalis*, the imaginal realm, the in between place between the material and spiritual worlds. The symbolic language of images, whether conjured up through dream, writing, visioning, or dancing, is perceived through the heart, not the rational brain. The heart is the doorway to the imaginal realm—the *mundus imaginalis,* because it is the organ that perceives images, according to the Sufi and other traditions.

Lillian, too, enters into the imaginal realm as she engages with her dream images through her medium of choice, painting. Images that emerge in dreams or visions are not limited to the personal unconscious but also arise from the collective unconscious (Jung C. G., Visions, 1997, p. xiii) as exemplified by Lillian's "snakes in the grass" and giant wave "hurricane" images. As her image sequence begins to unfold, Lillian's journey centers on opening into Feminine consciousness, expressed as the emergent *kundalini* serpent, through

---

228 In Weimar Germany, a sculpture memorializes Goethe's love for Hāfiz: Two chairs facing each other poised for a discussion that could only occur as an act of imagination because of the centuries between them. The interested reader is encouraged to venture further up this tributary, which leads to the same ocean in which Rumi swims. Like Rumi's, the work of Hāfiz is a beautiful expression of Sufi mysticism and addresses similar themes of Beloved and Lover.

her own unique individuation process, and ultimately through the birthing of her awakened Self, or in Christian terms, Christ consciousness. Her dream sequence is at once personal *and* collective. The sequence and progression of looking at Lillian's dream series, versus each image in isolation, greatly expands the meaning of the broader context of what's happening physically, psychically, and spiritually. In Lillian's remarkable dream series, we are able to witness the unfolding or evolution of Lillian's psyche as she successfully moves further along the individuation process, as Jung might say, or unveiling Sophia in the esoteric Christian or Sufi tradition. What emerged was a magnificent journey for both of us.

Plate 1 Snake Rising Up to Strike. A Second Snake is in the Grass, 10-24 2016

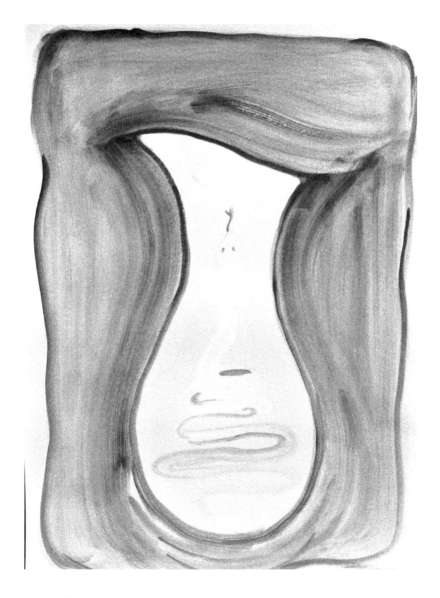

Plate 2 Snake in Alchemical Vessel, Fall 2016

Plate 3 Woman in Alchemical Vessel, 11-16-2016

Plate 4 Hurricane Dream, Part I, 11-19-2016

"I ride out a big hurricane in Charleston, South Carolina. I take refuge in a big church. The seaswells and waves batter the walls and windows of the church."

Plate 5 Hurricane Dream, Part 2, 11-20-2016

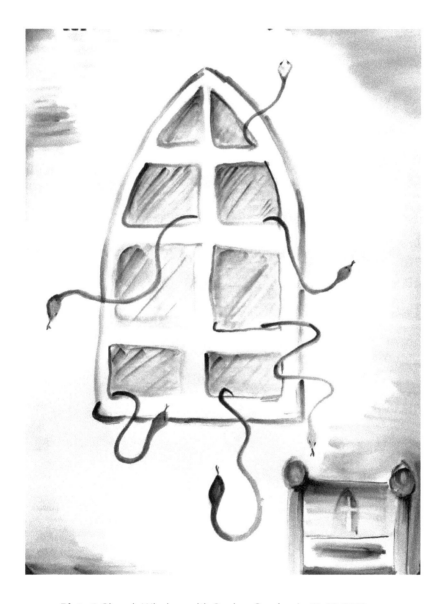

Plate 6 Church Window with Snakes Coming In, 11-22-2016

Plate 7 The Annunciation

Plate 8 Snake Dance, 12-13-2016

Plate I

> *"A snake is coming toward me with its mouth wide open as if it will strike. It strikes me and I awake with a violent start."*

From Lillian's above narrative, the snake is ready for an encounter, whereas she, the dreamer, is not. Lillian expressed that she had no idea what the snake "wanted," and its motivation was a mystery to her; "it pops out when she least expects it." She never knows if a snake is harmless or poisonous, and snakes frighten her with their hiddenness and with their unpredictable behavior.

At this initiatory point of the journey many people turn back because it requires probing into unknown and potentially dangerous places. The snake in Plate 1 is unambiguously vying for her attention and strikes; one possible way of engaging with this theme is that the snake is calling her, startling her out of a complacency that the ego prefers. Note that there is a second snake that appears in the grass; it is smaller, looking away, and horizontal in position. The juxtaposition of the two snakes may signal a shift from the mundane world of materiality to the spiritual dimension, whose intersection is at the heart where materiality and spirituality intersect. The number 2 holds significance in Jungian psychology and creation myths from Wisdom traditions.

The number 2 symbolizes coming into consciousness and out of the state of a unified whole. That which has emerged from the unitive source, the monad, and has now entered the realm of duality. The image of the snake itself plays a key role in many world mythologies, including world creation myths. The Christian Wisdom Tradition has the snake in the Garden of Eden that prompted Eve to entice Adam to partake of the apple. Depicted as evil, the snake shoulders the Feminine shadow as it was Eve who took the first bite. The snake does not appeal directly to Adam; rather, it utilizes the feminine to embody its intention.

In Christian iconography, and with the help of the patriarchy, Mary crushes the snake's head (primal feminine essence). There is a clear denial of the powerful archetypal qualities of the snake and its relation to the feminine. Cultures since antiquity, such as the Sumerians and Egyptians, honored the snake and the feminine. As the Christian Tradition teaches, the snake is synonymous with sin and Satan, and projects these negative attributes onto Eve and Mary from the Gospel of Mary. In like manner, Christianity has split Mary into good and evil, the virgin and the whore. Similarly, Sophia was decoupled from the word wisdom in many biblical passages, thus expunging this feminine form. This dissociation of the wholly/holy feminine has informed the Western psyche (whether or not one is Christian) to present times. The cultural context through which Westerners perceive the world has been impacted by the split between Madonna and Whore and the stark absence of the Feminine as a deity.

As previously mentioned, the important idea is to continue to work with the images and not concretize the process by assigning definitive meanings. The snake image evokes a multitude of associations, ranging from the so-called "evil" snake in the garden of Eden to the medical caduceus; essentially, its depths are unknowable, and the image will continue to "speak" as long as we let it. Therefore, I offer associations based on discussions with the dreamer, but not a definitive definition.

As we continue to explore Lillian's dream series unfolding, we see the greater context of this specific dream as the symbology plays out juxtaposed to images that follow. James Hillman's mantra, "stay with the image," is sage advice as we continue to explore and make associations while keeping the image as the central focus. By actively engaging with the image, it remains vibrant and continues living across cultural times adding to the collective pool.

Plate 2

The next image in the dream sequence (Plate 2) reveals a coiled snake rising upward in the rounded bottomed vessel. From a depth psychological perspective, the snake contained in a vessel infers that an alchemical process is proceeding. The snake is uncoiling and reaching vertically, and the horizontal plane has now been left behind.

The translucent green snake is surrounded by a container of white, which symbolizes the *albedo*[229] phase in alchemy. With a gentle and constant heat applied to the base of the rounded vessel, the process of "whitening" of the snake becomes apparent as it is now more translucent. *Albedo* (*ablutio*) is analogous to Sufi notion of the "cleaning of the mirror" through continuous prayer discussed earlier or *tapas* (inner heat) from the Tantric tradition where impurities are washed away. This image suggests a purification phase is potentially happening within the dreamer.

The broader background matrix holding the alchemical vessel is the color blue with darkening edges, signaling the alchemical transition from black to white. Blue in alchemy, as both Jung and Hillman pointed out, symbolizes vertical movement: "The vertical direction, as Jung reaffirms (CJV 12, para.320), is traditionally associated with blue." (http://www.pantheatre.com/pdf/6-reading-list-JH-blue.pdf). The snake's upright position further substantiates vertical dimensionality in the midst of blue. James Hillman has written extensively on alchemical color transformation and one of his associations of blue, pertinent to *Unveiling*, is with the "wisdom of Sophia"[230]; perhaps by this he meant a cosmological or abstract aspect.

Alchemically speaking, blue facilitates the transition from black to white and carries some of psyche's former dark *nigredo,* a deadening or descent to the underworld phase along with it.

> The purity of white does not come without its hefty price, and alchemical white is not of innocence; rather, it is hard won purity forged by the heat of fire. Whitening, *albedo*, is a stage of abstraction, and the process moves next to yellowing (*citrinitas*), which transforms silver into gold or the dawning of the solar light. The reddening (*rubeo*) marks a coming back into life and a return to consciousness.

---

229   (expand note) *Albedo* is one of the four major stages in the alchemical process, which follows black *nigredo*, and precedes yellow and red.

230   file:///Users/annetaylor16/Desktop/Alchemcial%20Blue_James%20Hillman.pdf

Plate 3

The next image Lillian presented underscores that a potent trans-formation is in process, as a woman appears in place of the snake, presumably, the dreamer herself. As a symbol of the creative life force, or *kundalini* that lies dormant at the base of the spine in both men and women, it appears that Lillian's *kundalini* may be psychically awakening or rising. This is perhaps a foreshadowing of her physical experiences to follow, which we will explore shortly. For the moment, the background color has transitioned sharply and now appears as muted earthy yellowish tones. The woman's hair is red, the alchemi-cal stage of *rubedo,* or reddening, a coming back into life phase. Her long red hair ends in spiral-like curves, reminiscent of the snake previously occupying the vessel. The white background in the vessel has darkened noticeably, and the outline of the vessel has become more pronounced. The egg-shaped white dots appear to be under the green earth. Again, this commentary is not designed to exhaust the image; rather engage with the primary images within their greater context. The dramatic transformation of her snake into human form signals the completion of one cycle (oscillation) of her individuation process. Lillian is now ready to dive "below the baseline of the sine wave" and pick up fresh archetypal images.

Plates 4 and 5

Lillian presented the "Hurricane Series" next, which followed later in the autumn of 2016. The dream images convey threatening conditions to an idyllic white church near the sea, thus signaling the initiation phase of the hero's journey where challenges are encountered. Plate 4 reveals three dominant blue waves crashing onto the side of the church and a fourth wave that appears somewhat recessive and farthest from the church. From a depth psychological viewpoint, the ocean sym-bolizes the unconscious psyche, and something deep within Lillian's psyche appears to be rising up, perhaps to challenge the status quo of the church. I suggest this, in part, because of an impactful book that Lillian shared with me, *The Dance of the Dissident Daughter: A Woman's Journey from Christian Tradition to the Sacred Feminine* (Kidd, 1996). Sue Monk Kidd's journey leads us through her journey of recovering the lost feminine in an arena of conventional patriarchal Christianity. Kidd, like Lillian, sought to lift the veil of Sophia.

The waves appear as spinal formations, potentially overlapping symbolism with the previous coiled snake images, or another association is simply the spiral movement of nature. Appearing in the sky is an exaggerated waxing crescent moon, a traditional alchemical symbol of the feminine (Luna), contrasted to the golden sun as masculine (Sol). The young (but growing) feminine silvery moon coupled with the blue waves brings us once again to the transitional state between the black *nigredo* sky and the white church. There is movement and psychic processing stirring, which continues to escalate as we move to Plate 5.

In Plate 5, there again are three waves of a blue-green color crashing into the side of the church; however, the fourth wave appears to have now emerged into a prominent position. It is far more powerful, darker, larger than the other waves and reaches *under* the church. The feeling tone of Plate 5 is threatening, as if the fourth wave is ready to uproot the church from its foundation. Notice the darker and larger fourth wave appears to be undermining the church; perhaps the dreamer's psyche is calling for her to reconsider some of her assumptions about what she has been taught by the Church. The movement from 3 to 4 may provide some clues, perhaps an expansion requiring her to move beyond the Trinity to a Jungian quaternity of completion.

What does a quaternity look like in terms of Christianity, the dreamer's spiritual tradition? We will pick up this thread again shortly, but first let us look further into the fourth wave.

Something substantial is growing under the surface of the church that is no longer willing or able to be suppressed. There is a fourth element that was latent in Plate 4 and has now emerged. Jung contended that the number 3 indicates psychic movement along the path of completion; however the process remains incomplete until the "fourth" emerges. Inferring from Lillian's earlier snake sequence, it may be the emerging dark feminine or Black Madonna (feminine divine earth spirit) (snake and dark powerful wave) that is about to bring her to her next stage of wholeness. The feminine archetype is not always a nurturing and gentle one; she has a counterbalance of destructive power and force to be used when it is necessary to dismantle and rebirth that which no longer serves. Mother Nature exemplifies this, as does the goddess Kali from the Hindu tradition.

Traditions such as Hinduism do not shy away from the dark feminine archetype as Christianity does. Kali, *Kālikā* translates to "the deep blue one," an aspect of the Divine Mother who has come to destroy evil and to evoke changes needed over time, a natural and necessary phase of evolution. Kali wears a necklace of skulls and dances upon her consort, Shiva. She is the fierce side of Adi Shakti, Mother of the Universe, who will kill to protect.

The archetypal feminine, in all of her faces, appears to be a common theme through Lillian's dream series. Before returning to the dream images, the significance of moving from 3 to 4 will now be further explored in more detail in order to more fully appreciate the dreamer's emerging symbolism.

Transitioning from 3 to 4

The significance of the relationship between 3 and 4 dates back to antiquity, and likely beyond, as Plato's opening question in *Timaeus* (circa 428 B.C.E.-347 B.C.E.) begins: "One, two, three—but where, my dear Timaeus, is the fourth of our guests of yesterday, our hosts of to- day?" (p. 17) Does Plato intend to simply be counting off guests, or is he likely speaking in symbolic language? Food for thought; let's continue. Jungian psychology teaches that 3 is the number of resolution, the trinity for example, which represents a synthesis to the conflict between polar opposites, or the number 2. Jung refers to the processing of 2 to 3 as the "transcendent function." This "third thing" comes from beyond the logic of the mind, and in a sense it represents a solution to a seemingly insurmountable problem that comes "out of the blue."

Jung viewed the alchemical axiom of Maria Propetissa, "Out of the One comes Two, out of Two comes Three, and from the Third comes the One as the Fourth,[231]" as a model for the individuation process. In other words, as the psychic process successfully proceeds from 1 to 2, 2 to 3, and 3 to 4, a new wholeness has been achieved, which brings about the birth of a transformed human being, and thus back to 1 for the process to begin anew. By this point in Jung's life, he was getting quite old and passed the torch to Marie Louise von Franz to further develop his theory that natural integers are the archetypal energies that regulate psyche and matter, relating back to the *unus mundus* (Latin for one world), or in today's terminology, unified field. Interested readers are encouraged to read von Franz's *Number and Time* (von Franz, 1974). Referring back to Section I, HRV was represented as numbers links psyche and soma. Lillian's dreams also articulate the significance of numbers relating to one's psychic process.

Transitioning from 3 to 4 is difficult because it also involves a surrender of ego to the higher authority of the Self. Jung wrote extensively about 4 as the archetype of psychic wholeness, and the transition from 3 to 4 is a significant part of one's journey to wholeness. The transition from 3 to 4 is not limited to Jungian psychology, including its Platonic lineage.

The model of the Tantric chakra system[232] exemplifies the challenge of transitioning from 3 to 4 in its model of consciousness, the chakra system. The third *chakra* at the navel (*manipura*) is separated from the fourth, or heart chakra (*anahata*), by a psycho-spiritual "knot" (*granthi*) with a physical basis. One must break through or untie the "knot of Vishnu," which lies between the third chakra at the naval and the fourth chakra (*anahata*) at the heart center. From a subtle energetic standpoint, when the knot of Vishnu is untied, the *kundalini* energy is free to continue her passage up the *Sushumna nadi*, the central subtle energy channel aligned with the spinal

---

231 https://en.wikipedia.org/wiki/Axiom_of_Maria

232 *Kundalini* yoga is derived from the Tantric chakra system that typically refers to the sevenenergy wheels (*chakras*) or vortices that align with the spine, each with its specific level of consciousness.

column. Untying the knot symbolically encapsulates the battle of shifting from will/ego to heart, to a life based on humility and compassion—a purified heart. Considerable psychic and physical energy is needed to transform a life lived from the egoic mind (third *chakra*) to a life based on heart-centered living with the Self as the central controlling power (fourth *chakra*). This is a yogic challenge as well as one of individuation.

We shall now return to Lillian's dream images and continue to see what unfold.

Plate 6

In Plate 6, we again see a dramatic shift as Lillian's next image reveals snakes coming out of several of the church's windows, although it is unclear what happened to the rest of the church after the hurricane. Windows may be associated with light or stages of consciousness, particularly when presented in association with a church. The Eros, or power of the dark fourth wave, has unleashed the snakes, whose images are now freely moving in and around the church window. The energy has ascended, can no longer be contained. The key recurring images are: Winding Snake(s), Church, Window, Ascending. The mandorla-shaped window will also appear in in Lillian's final image in the series. The archetypal eternal feminine snake is moving things forward, or "hithers us on," as Goethe phrased it.

Plate 7

Plate 7, titled "Snake dance," shows another dramatic turn as the woman appears for the first time in the same image as the snake. She's dancing with the snake and appears to be somewhat ecstatic or possibly entranced. The snake still has its mouth wide open, yet the woman is now in control as she holds the snake above her head and out of danger. Victory, with both arms up reaching to the heavens, she exudes and communicates triumph. Originally threatened by the snake, she has transformed its primal creative potential into her own feminine power. It is important to note that Lillian did not reject the snake; rather, she allowed it to become part of her creative process.

This point is underscored by Lillian's own nonreactive or calm response to her physical sensations of apparent *kundalini* rising within her daytime reality.

Plate 8 "The Annunciation"
(Return Phase of the Hero's Journey)

Lillian titled the final dream image "Annunciation" and now marks the return phase of her heroine's journey. Archetypes often present themselves as archetypal images in the cultural dress familiar to the dreamer or visioner. As a Christian woman, the Feast of the Annunciation is familiar to her, and she understands the significance of St. Gabriel appearing to Mary:

Hail, full of grace, the Lord is with you! (Lk 1:28)

Mary consented to the Incarnation of the Son of God within her body by responding, "Let it be." There is a necessary surrender of personal ego to that which is higher within. As the visioner, Lillian is filled with this image, the image of her own divinity within. She now stands with her angel or the angelic aspect of herself—a form of Mary, Sophia, the divine Feminine archetype. Both figures appear to be floating on the rippling water. The dove flies above, symbolic of the Holy Spirit or risen *kundalini* energy. She is contained and held within the mandorla shape, which Lillian associates with Christ, the intermediary between human and divine. From a Jungian perspective, this phase of her individuation process is complete or moving toward completion. The halo or auric fields around the heads of both figures are expansive. The crescent moon in Plate 4 is now depicted in its full ripeness, signaling her expanded sacred feminine or Sophia consciousness, the Feminine aspect of Christ.

At the top of the image, a double quaternity or dual mandala appears with one prominent cross and a smaller secondary one, looking much like a nautical compass symbol. There is a cosmic or celestial component to the angelic figure mirroring Lillian and suggests that she herself has completed an important phase in her individuation process, spiritual in nature. This possibility becomes more viable based on an observation that Lillian shared more than one year after the dream sequence and shortly after her physiological-spiritual *kundalini* awakening experience.

2-22-2018 Post-Dream Correspondence

Lillian writes: "I had a sort of mini-awakening yesterday and I am feeling a bit vulnerable and afraid today. The mini awakening came in this form. I was reading Christian scripture about the heart and about wisdom [Sophia]. In the past, scripture has never made sense to me. It always seemed abstruse and maybe even irrelevant. Yesterday the passages I read suddenly made perfect sense. I saw that these people who wrote the words knew wisdom and knew the heart. They knew what they were talking about! This change in perception brought to mind the words of that hymn 'Amazing Grace' which go[es] 'I was blind but now I see.' I felt energized but also somewhat afraid regarding this change in my perception."

Lillian's ability to suddenly understand symbolic biblical passages that previously seemed meaningless was understandably a bit unsettling to her, however it was the fruitful conclusion of this portion of her spiritual journey or individuation process. One hallmark of spiritual progress is the attainment of humility, as one brushes up against Universal consciousness or the ineffable divine. The culmination of her experiences resulted in her obtaining Sophic wisdom—she lifted the veil of Sophia.

Printed in the USA
CPSIA information can be obtained
at www.ICGtesting.com
JSHW070213090324
58848JS00017B/122